the 21st century office
Jeremy Myerson and Philip Ross

the 21st century office

architecture and design for the new millennium

Jeremy Myerson and Philip Ross

Rizzoli NEW YORK

First published in the United States of America in 2003 by
Rizzoli International Publications, Inc.
300 Park Avenue South
New York, NY 10010
www.rizzoliusa.com

Distributed to the U.S. trade by St. Martin's Press, New York

This book was produced by Laurence King Publishing Ltd, London
www.laurenceking.co.uk

Text © 2003 Jeremy Myerson and Philip Ross

2003 2004 2005 2006 2007/ 10 9 8 7 6 5 4 3 2 1

Library of Congress Control Number: 2003101220

ISBN 0-8478-2552-3 Softcover

Designed by Price Watkins
Edited by Henrietta Heald

Printed in Singapore

contents

1 narrative

2 nodal

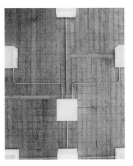

Ceiling grid, Philipp and Keuntje, Hamburg

The Tube, Ogilvy & Mather, Los Angeles

3 **neighbourly**

4 **nomadic**

Globe chair, Virgin Atlantic, New York

Duck lights, Beacon, Tokyo

introduction

THE office as we know it today is a relatively new phenomenon. It dominates the working lives of hundreds of millions of people yet it dates back little more than 100 years. As the physical setting for the necessary functions that support industry, business and government, the office can be described as one of the key societal landmarks of the 20th century. It has exerted a profound influence not just on economic development but also on culture, lifestyle, environment and the urban landscape.

The office in the 20th century followed the now well-understood path of modernization and technological advance. One hundred years ago, the dawn of a new century acted as the catalyst for a cluster of new inventions – among them the lightbulb, elevator, telephone and typewriter – that revolutionized the world of work within dedicated office buildings. Many of these buildings were high rise, the result of new construction techniques, and set in expanding city-centre business districts. But what of the 21st-century workplace?

Today, many of the economic imperatives, social attitudes and dominant technologies that drove the development of the scientifically managed 20th-century office have changed. In the early 20th century, a pattern was set that gradually obliged the workforce to commute to the city from the surburbs or other outlying areas. The scale and complexity of the office grew to the point at which it became a high-tech box for facilitating work – the result of an alliance of management efficiency theory, systemic modern design and bulky, tethered technology.

But workplace occupiers, architects and designers are no longer following the same rules. In fact, the thrust of this book is that a new 21st-century office is emerging which represents a complete reassessment of everything previously understood about the traditional architectural container for white-collar work. Another cluster of inventions – the internet, email and mobile telephony, in particular – is having a similarly catalytic effect on office interiors of the early 21st century, creating a new paradigm.

The 21st Century Office presents the first overview of the workplaces that will set some of the trends for the next 100 years. In selecting and analysing 45 case studies from nine countries (China, Germany, Italy, Japan, The Netherlands, Spain, Sweden, UK and USA), we have charted a shift towards a new corporate consensus about workplace design – one that supersedes the territorial values, supervisory cultures and economies of scale that helped to define the 20th-century office.

1 concept: narrative

client Sweden Post **location** Stockholm, Sweden **designer** MVRDV **total floor space** 22,500 square metres (242,200 square feet)

This competition entry by Dutch designers MVRDV relocates the former state-owned Sweden Post from a traditional headquarters with cellular offices and endless corridors to a dramatic new setting, which tells a story about its transformation into a private commercial company. The scheme sets the new headquarters in a fictional 'North Park', using the local topology of forested hills and lakes to build a narrative about the national heritage of Sweden Post. The working environment is literally integrated into the hillside terraces, harmonizing nature and technology and making us reassess what the office building of the 21st century could look like.

This process of change has been in motion for some time. In 1999 we wrote a book entitled *The Creative Office*, which suggested that the consensus about the 20th-century corporate workplace was breaking down. Several schemes showed how large mainstream companies were fast adopting alternative ways to redesign their offices that had once been the exclusive preserve of smaller, more agile, creative-industry firms. This search for new ideas reflected a sign of deep disenchantment with conventional workplace design.

The central message of *The Creative Office* was that fixed, sterile, factory-floor office environments could no longer support new styles of team-based, knowledge-driven, community-oriented working, nor the demands of an increasingly mobile and self-deterministic workforce. Three years on, *The 21st Century Office* presents not so much an amplification of those first signs of change but a real shift of architectural and organizational approach.

A fundamental review

It is not that the office interior is itself on the way to becoming obsolete, even though more work than ever before is being done outside the conventional corporate workplace. On the contrary, office buildings remain important organizational anchors. However, our research suggests that property and space are beginning to be treated in a new and different way. In particular, four of the most basic features of the 20th-century office – its visual uniformity and banality, operational inflexibility, lack of human interaction and place-dependency – are now being subjected to wide-ranging review. The four key themes of *The 21st Century Office* – Narrative, Nodal, Neighbourly and Nomadic – shine a light on those aspects of 20th-century working life that are currently being replaced, sidelined or transformed.

The Narrative office represents a powerful reaction against the anonymous-looking, automated, over-engineered workplaces of the past 40 years. From the 1960s onwards, offices were designed to be blandly neutral, first by risk-averse developers, and then by corporate tenants who adopted 'vanilla' solutions driven by global standards that dictated everything from the colour of the carpet to the size of an office for a particular grade of worker. The lowest common denominator became the easiest design solution to implement, and a neutral, benign aesthetic of endless repetition crept into the workplace.

In accommodating the relentless demands of technology, all offices started to look alike. Was it a tax accountant or an ad agency? You couldn't tell the nature of the business from the standard configurations of open workstations on cable-managed floors before your eyes. The office interior rarely betrayed the inner workings of the company or revealed its brands or products.

That neutral approach – brilliantly parodied in the hit British TV comedy *The Office* starring Ricky Gervais – is now also under sustained attack from designers. The case studies in the Narrative section of this book describe a new approach in which office environments are no longer blank boxes for work – they tell a story about a company and its brands through a 'narrative experience' or journey through interior space.

The Nodal office is a response to the inflexible, isolating culture of 20th-century headquarters buildings as hierarchical containers for work, populated by largely sedentary workforces unable to share ideas with clients or colleagues on account of the status-driven, departmental, static division of space. By the early 1990s, office occupation studies revealed that larges swathes of valuable real estate were being left unused for most of the day, with an average 60 per cent of workstations lying empty at any point in time, as more mobile, 'drop-in' workstyles evolved.

New ways of working such as 'hot desking' and 'hoteling' were introduced, but many such space-sharing initiatives became crude exercises in reducing the size of office floors and saving money, resulting in organizational instability and staff hostility. In the digital age, when people increasingly pass through the office on a need basis or connect to it remotely, a new approach is required; also, teams use the space for defined projects, and clients are encouraged to participate and 'immerse' themselves rather than act as passive spectators.

The Nodal case studies describe imaginative new offices that provide a fixed point in an increasingly virtual world, offering a resource for networking, coaching, training and sharing knowledge – places where people interact and into which employees and external collaborators alike can plug.

The Neighbourly office is a vibrant reaction against the command-and-control legacy of the 20th-century office, which created suspicion and hostility between supervisors and staff – and undermined attempts to create social communities of purpose in the workplace.

The earliest modern offices forbade conversation and frowned on social contact, enshrining the work ethic in the dull monotony of the work aesthetic. But, as office work passed through its factory-based, paper-processing phase towards a more collaborative and cognitive mode requiring team-generation of ideas, many organizations began to count the cost of negative human relations.

The office of the last century was designed to keep people apart – a division of labour. Now the office is increasingly designed to encourage the chance encounters from which good ideas flow. A growing debate about a better work–life balance for employees and changing demographics, which will see increasing numbers of older people remain in the workforce as the age of eligibility for the state pension rises, have also begun to influence a new focus on comfort, congeniality and community in the office. The Neighbourly case studies show a repertoire of creative strategies to encourage social interaction, many of them based on the idea of the city plan.

The Nomadic office represents the logical conclusion of a technology-driven trend to liberate work from the workplace. For most of the 20th century, the office was fixed in time, place and space. People commuted to and from office buildings at set hours. The only way of contacting a company was by physically connecting to its buildings by phone or facsimile, or by writing a letter to its postal address. Now people can work anywhere they choose and the corporate 'address' is no longer represented by bricks and mortar.

Work stretches across a continuum of locations, from home and high street to transport hub and serviced club – wherever people need to be. The predictable working day is being replaced by a 24/7 culture in which people are connected to the organization and its clients from wherever they are. The Nomadic projects in this book reflect that approach. They show useful new workplaces springing up within social housing, rural villages, motorway service stations and airports.

Early adopters
Who are the early adopters of these trends? The Narrative approach showcased in *The 21st Century Office* is dominated by large brand manufacturers – the global players such as Toyota, Sony, Reebok and Quiksilver – although small architecture and design firms have also become adept at building a storyline about their practice. The Nodal office has been pioneered mainly by management consultants and technology companies who want to create experience and learning environments.

2 concept: nodal

client IT Fornebu Eiendom **location** Oslo, Norway **designer** Aviaplan **total floor space** 40,000 square metres (430,500 square feet)

When Oslo international airport was relocated to a site north of the city, the old terminal, apron and ancillary buildings were sold for development. This project reinvents the airport terminal as an IT and innovation centre – an archetypal Nodal office of the 21st century containing research, conference, education and training facilities as well as an incubator centre to develop new business ideas. With its glazed circulation routes and many different meeting spaces, the scheme focuses on knowledge exchange and connection – equalizing the disparity between large and small companies – and on providing the right mix of work and social facilities where and when they are needed.

Neighbourly offices are currently the domain of advertising agencies and marketing services companies who want to build creative communities, and call centres who want to reduce high levels of staff turnover. Nomadic spaces are to some extent independent of companies, and are created by the organizations who own or operate corporate associations and transportation hubs. These are the clubs, guilds and services that will knit together the geographically distributed workplace of the new century. Nomadic is about the local community and working at home, as well as the places in between.

From neutral to Narrative

The Narrative office has powerful 20th-century precedents. IBM was famous for its signature approach to real estate worldwide. Buildings as diverse as the Chrysler Building in New York, the Hoover Building in London and the Fiat factory in Turin set up a strong narrative in the visitor's mind. But, as Wallis Gilbert's Art Deco fantasy for Hoover on London's Great West Road showed, behind the façade it was generally business as usual. The storyline was only skin deep.

What is so striking about the new cluster of Narrative office projects is the commitment to making the office environment a substantive tool in the business of brand differentiation. In a world of similarly priced and tightly legislated service industries, where companies struggle to find the clear technological point of difference enjoyed by companies 50 or more years ago, this will increasingly be the case. Even car makers struggle to define their own corner, given the similarities of the modern aerodynamically designed saloon.

Inside a Narrative office, you 'live and breathe' the brand, whether you are skating across a polished 'beachfront boardwalk' inside the Quiksilver headquarters designed by

Bauer and Wiley (pages 18–23), lunching next to a gleaming new model parked in the 'main street' of Toyota's UK headquarters designed by Sheppard Robson (pages 78–83), or jogging around the running track that forms an integral part of the new Reebok campus designed by NBBJ (pages 66–71).

This approach reflects the view that marketing is no longer a discrete function – all office staff are perceived to be in the marketing front-line, and the spaces in which they work have become prime platforms to communicate brand ethos all day long. As Paul Brown, vice president of product design at Reebok, remarked of his new building just outside Boston: 'Products, innovation, marketing ... what we've achieved here is a perfect synergy. This is our church. Everything that comes out of our church represents what we do. When you come into the building you know what you do and who you are.'

Some Narrative offices have compelling introductions to establish the plot. Ogilvy & Mather's new office in Los Angeles (pages 28–33) sets up its fresh storyline with a journey through a perforated metal 'time tunnel'; Bloomberg's base in London's Finsbury Square (pages 56–61) takes you up through a darkened lobby as hidden cameras transfer your silhouette onto a light frieze. Others trade on the creative tension between seeming opposites. Allsteel (pages 74–77), for example, adopts rural, homespun Midwestern motifs to convey contemporary style for an Iowa-based furniture brand; architect Fuksas Associati (pages 72–73) blends antiquity and modernity in the interiors of a much-renovated 16th-century Roman *palazzo*; Japanese legend Issey Miyake (pages 44–47) unravels a story of fashion individuality in the neutral open spaces of a speculative Tokyo office block.

What characterizes all Narrative offices is a sense of playfulness and surprise – from the Sony Playstation symbols (cross, triangle, etc) hidden in the company's European

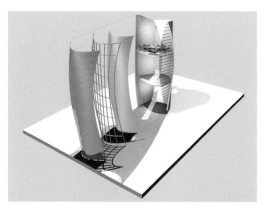

headquarters in London (pages 24–27) to the US-style mailboxes that turn up on the 'main street' of Vitra's office in Weil am Rhein, Germany (pages 34–39). Sometimes the surprise is huge: Frank Gehry's monumental DZ Bank building in Berlin (pages 48–53) reveals a sculptural conference chamber in its main atrium space that is menacingly shaped like a giant prehistoric horse's skull to symbolize the enduring power of financial services. Sometimes it is more subtly sprung, as in the circular motifs (from panel perforations to rotundas) that evoke the music turntable in Muzak's South Carolina headquarters (pages 40–43).

Whatever the creative strategy, the Narrative trend is a way to banish the bland office interior – by linking the interior journey through the space to the fictional aspect of the brand itself. Taken to an extreme – as in the concept shown on pages 8–9, which creates a fictional hillside location for a new headquarters for Sweden Post – the Narrative office has the potential to rethink the 21st-century office building through the process of defining and reinforcing brand values.

From narrow to Nodal

The Nodal office is predicated on the effects of digital technology and thus has far fewer 20th-century precedents. A key element of this trend is workplaces that are much more flexible, especially in terms of creating environments for education and training. 'Client outreach' is the new phrase to describe the role of Nodal spaces in bringing companies and their customers together for corporate knowledge-sharing. Projects for IBM's e-business in Santa Monica (pages 116–19) and PricewaterhouseCoopers in Philadelphia (pages 100–103) both present a themed set of richly choreographed spaces to enhance this process. The static demonstration room in which companies try to make the sale is becoming a thing of the past.

Nodal environments have elements of the Narrative approach. Often, scripted or programmed multimedia experiences offer clients a mix of education and entertainment that informs as well as creating an impression. Winstar in New York (pages 90–95) and Media Plaza in Utrecht (pages 110–15) both give digital services a compelling physical presence. Valtech in London (pages 96–99) meanwhile adopts an *Alice in Wonderland* metaphor to spring its surprises in a training environment of giant photomurals and secret doors.

The ability of Nodal offices to 'incubate' new ideas by providing a range of spaces in which to generate, test and share them is reflected in an innovative scheme for McKinsey & Co in Amsterdam harbour (pages 86–89), with its mix of 'lounges' and 'cocoons'. Oliver, Wyman in New York breaks the mould of impersonal hot desking to create a more engaging base for its highly mobile workforce of financial consultants (pages 104–109).

The Wyman project's generous zoning and circulation, together with the mix of Nodal spaces in a converted parish hall for Philipp and Keuntje in Hamburg (pages 126–29), suggest that the formula for shared space in the new century will be much less pared-down and penny-pinching than in the past. Consultants will no longer have to get in early to grab a space.

Indeed, the conceptual designs shown on pages 10–11 for Norway's IT Fornebu Eiendom – which transform the old Oslo airport into a drop-in centre for research, training, conferencing and business incubation – illustrate just how far the Nodal trend can stretch in the near future.

From negative to Neighbourly

Just as the pioneer offices of the early 20th century were driven by the metaphor of the machine (Mies van der Rohe once famously described the workplace as 'a machine for

3 concept: neighbourly

client *Business Week* magazine **project** Office of the 21st Century **designer** Charles Rose Architects

This concept scheme was commissioned by *Business Week* as part of a special issue on the 21st-century corporation. It describes the future workplace as having a number of defining characteristics, most notably a generosity of social space with transparent meeting rooms devoid of technology to reinforce face-to-face contact and dialogue. This idea of the office as a social landscape is reinforced by a blurring of the distinction between inside and outside: gardens form part of the work environment and fibrous-membrane interior walls support hydroponic plants. Individual work shells provide private enclosures but can be grouped into neighbourly clusters for open team working.

working in'), the Neighbourly office of the early 21st century is driven by the metaphor of the club or the city – as a large, colourful place of social activity and interaction.

Architect Clive Wilkinson was among the first to define the office as a social landscape with his scheme for TBWA\Chiat\Day in Los Angeles (pages 192–97), which models the agency on a neighbourhood of Manhattan's Greenwich Village, complete with streets, cars, parks, baseball court and dwellings. Another Californian advertising agency project by Wilkinson – this time for Foote, Cone & Belding (pages 132–37) – reinterprets the social office quarter as a harbourside that is metaphorically poised between land and sea.

Advertising agencies make willing clients for Neighbourly office projects. An organizational type that once bristled with Madison Avenue-style corporate self-importance has discovered a refreshing sense of adventure – and a sense of humour – in its contemporary approach to interior design. Both Beacon in Tokyo (pages 168–73) and Claydon Heeley Jones Mason in London (pages 184–87) have adopted the device of the ribbon to create accessible, free-flowing effects in their environments. Beacon's commitment to social cohesion even extends to a long directors' dining table with friendly duck lights, to which any employee can pull up a chair.

Other companies accentuate a sense of community in different ways – from another.com's 'surf and turf' strategy (employees can stretch out on a real grass lawn inside the office – pages 138–41) to Planungsgruppe Drahtler's showstopping 'red box' in the centre of its Dortmund office (pages 188–91). Few organizations, however, can match the commitment to fun exhibited by London agency Exposure, whose multicultural sense of neighbourliness is reflected in the 'walk through the markets of the world' that describes its eclectic interiors.

Indeed, if California pioneered the office as social landscape, then the UK is catching on fast. Even in the call-centre sector, which has been dubbed 'the sweatshop of the 21st century', operator-friendly schemes by Richard Hywel Evans for Cellular Operations in Swindon (pages 162–67) and by DEGW for Egg in Derby (pages 174–79) show what can be achieved with creative imagination and a bold client.

From nesting to Nomadic

The Nomadic office describes a series of geographically distributed spaces for work. Collectively, these schemes represent the most radical departure from the location-dependent office of the 20th century. Some work settings are based around transport hubs or systems, such as Workspace, a joint venture by Granada Service Stations and BT which creates a Nomadic work destination for 'road warriors' on Britain's main motorways (pages 226–27).

Airlines, too, have realized that, in the highly competitive world of aviation, business travellers require more attractive, conducive and exclusive workspaces within airports to remain loyal. Many business lounges are being transformed from glorified bars to sophisticated environments for working on the move – as smartly designed schemes for Virgin Atlantic in New York's JFK airport (pages 214–17) and Cathay Pacific in Hong Kong's Chep Lap Kok airport (pages 224–25) suggest.

Indeed, the alternatives to taking out a long lease on an expensive office are growing in an increasingly nomadic world of work. You can spend your time in a business club such as the Institute of Directors in London, whose IoD at 123 (pages 200–205) provides a strikingly contemporary series of work settings for nomadic executives as well as services, food and drink. You can make your home a really creative and

connected office – even if it is situated in a remote 12th-century Italian hilltop village (pages 222–23). Or you can rent upmarket serviced office space in a flagship building, without the large overhead that is normally concealed behind the impressive front door, as the Ocubis project in London's Knightbridge demonstrates (pages 218–21).

The Nomadic trend has the potential to turn the office into something else entirely. Fittingly, the final project in the book, Gallery-S in Japan, shows an office so light, transparent and 'dematerialized' that it doubles as an art gallery at weekends. Future concepts for Nomadic spaces will further dissolve the distinction between space and function. The concept scheme shown below for Domain, a designers' club in London, crosses the office with nightclub, blurring the boundaries between work and leisure, public and private. Commissioned by a group of film production companies as a special place for their nomadic workforce of freelancers to meet, it hints at a 21st-century equivalent of the work quarters set up by medieval craft guilds.

Cross-thematic trends

The Narrative, Nodal, Neighbourly and Nomadic trends are not mutually exclusive; indeed they share several governing characteristics. Throughout the case studies we have identified new approaches to office space. Gone are the linear corridors of old, the arterial roads of the corporate office that transported people efficiently from A to B. They have been replaced by the meandering lanes, boulevards and streets that bring people together and create the serendipitous meetings on which new business thrives.

If the 20th-century office promoted the value of workspace over public space, the new order is elevating social space, especially gathering and client meeting areas, as a premium investment. The hotel lobby, the gallery and the nightclub interior are all being mined for a new look that achieves a more people-centred effect. Perimeter circulation is a feature of several schemes.

The visit to most organizations used to end at the reception desk or in a closed-off meeting room. Now journeys through work environments are encouraged and choreographed. 'Experience' settings immerse visitors in the culture and process of the company, and new forms of managing people through spaces have been developed. Tunnels are used to funnel people through an environment; circulation has been transformed from the predictable passage to the unpredictable journey where surprising juxtapositions, angles and materials are combined to make people think again and challenge the basic assumptions they hold about office work.

Materials are no longer the neutral and functional backdrop to office life. They can dynamically project brand values, as in the abundance of low-tech birch and ply in Quiksilver's headquarters, or the 'honest' use of exposed concrete and ducting in Allsteel's Iowa showroom to reflect a no-nonsense approach. There is a move away from technological finishes to natural ones, with the curved, slatted wooden wall a feature of several schemes. Generally, the accent is less on status (marble finishes, expensive panelling, etc) and more on stage set (translucent acrylic panels, medium-density fibreboard, etc) that creates an effect and can be changed easily and relatively cheaply. The 21st-century office is about building communication, not monuments.

In this process, colour has a stronger role to play, banishing the beiges and greys of 20th-century corporatism. The palette is muted and sophisticated in some schemes: IBM, Happy Forsman & Bodenfors and Issey Miyake explore different shades of whiteness, finding an original angle on the 'vanilla solution'.

4 concept: nomadic

client Domain **location** London, UK **designer** Richard Hywel Evans Architecture and Design **total floor space** 740 square metres (8,000 square feet)

This innovative scheme for a designers' club in Soho, London, was commissioned by a group of film production companies who wanted a special public place for their nomadic workforce of freelancers to get together. The project proposes a club room for people from the same industry to touch down, socialize, eat and work. Interior spaces are graded from semi-public to confidential. 'Eat–work pods' are designed for non-confidential encounters; 'four-poster' spaces are transparent but provide complete audio privacy. This is a concept that crosses the office with nightclub, blurring the boundaries between work and play, public and private.

But many other offices make a feature of vibrant colour – from Bloomberg's coloured glazed screens that stretch up the building to Valtech's technicoloured fantasyland.

One of the clear trends from the case studies is the rise of the laptop computer, replacing the once ubiquitous personal computer (PC) on the desktop. Flat screens have signalled the end of the L-shaped desk, with its deep corner designed to accommodate a bulky monitor. Email and the internet, alongside its internal cousin, the intranet, are transforming corporate communication, while cell phones have rendered the old rules obsolete as a new generation becomes familiar with mobile telephony and the concept of being always in touch. The era of a telephone tethered to furniture – where you dialled a desk rather than a person – is coming to an end.

Wireless technology

Many companies have adopted wireless technology that makes it possible to connect a laptop to the network from anywhere in the building. This is key in allowing people to work in different places in the office, divorced from the umbilical cord that is the ethernet cable. Untethered, workers are choosing to use brand-new settings for tasks previously confined to the workstation. Cafés, sofas and lounge areas have become a connected part of the workplace. Even enclosed outdoor space has been effectively adopted as the office.

Other technologies, here now or just around the corner, will further drive these trends. Smaller, more portable devices will be tomorrow's productivity tools, enabling new workspaces to be used by people who bring their own technology. Personal digital assistants (PDAs), the Tablet PC, desktop projection, unified messaging and the wireless internet are some of the innovations that will accelerate the emergence of the 21st-century office.

Meanwhile, the technology-driven potential for 'place-independent' and nomadic work will be allied to growing environmental concerns about air conditioning, building energy use, car emissions, planning problems for new offices, the threat to the green belt, traffic congestion in towns and cities, and the relentless pressure on the transport infrastructure. The question will be asked: why should an entire working population be on the move at the same time each morning?

Attitudes to work and employment will also play their part. While previous generations expected to have jobs for life, the inhabitants of the 21st-century office will have been brought up on insecurity and short-term contracts. Future generations will not expect contracts at all, developing instead 'portfolio' careers in a freelance economy. They will be more mobile, more educated, better informed, and influenced by a proliferation of media and choices. They will no longer abide by the old 40/40 contract (40 hours a week for 40 years) and will expect a better deal in terms of work–life balance.

We believe that the four key trends identified in this book will develop and grow in their own right. Most of the case studies included here concentrate on organizations in discrete sectors such as media, advertising, management consultancy and technology. But we anticipate that these early adopters will surely influence the mainstream, especially if the benefits to be derived from new workplace innovation can win over the business sceptics.

What is increasingly clear to us is that an empowered workforce will vote with its feet. This is borne out by the experience of a number of the companies in this book who have been able to recruit and retain the right staff because 21st-century professionals want to work in 21st-century offices – not in the bland, tethered, inflexible and unloved boxes of old.

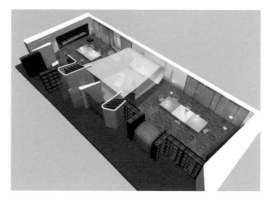

1 narrative

office as brand experience

Offices were once designed as blank boxes that betrayed little of the inner life of an organization. Most workplaces looked neutral and seemed identical. But, in the service-oriented economy of the 21st century, characterful new offices are emerging that are narrative in form – they tell a story about a company and its brand through an experience or journey through interior space. As branding and reputation become inextricably linked, offices acquire a powerful sense of identity in the eyes of their occupiers. The narrative office brings brand values alive, acts as a receptacle for corporate 'memory' and gives employees constant visual stimuli in their environment to promote a service ethos. Here is a selection of office interiors that illustrate the narrative trend.

Quiksilver
Newport Beach, California, USA
Bauer and Wiley

18 QUIKSILVER is the undisputed brand leader in fashionable surfing and skateboarding apparel. For 20 years, despite fickle market trends, its logo has been synonymous with surfboard style. So when the company decided to build a corporate headquarters next door to its distribution centre at Huntingdon Beach in Southern California, it made sense that the new workplace should be modelled on a 'small beach community'.

The resulting project by architects Bauer and Wiley expertly captures the essence of the Quiksilver brand in a series of confident metaphorical gestures. A polished 'boardwalk', for example, which bisects the interior from the front entrance to the distribution centre at the rear, is lined with a slatted birch treatment reminiscent of 'beach shacks'. Four towers that provide a conduit for technical services to enter the building are styled as lifeguard stands.

For all the laid-back, beachfront imagery, formed using a palette of honest, low-tech materials, this is a hard-working office solution. The designers were briefed to create a dynamic environment for a young, hip workforce with an average age of 24 without making the 'suits' (investors, bankers) feel uncomfortable. The budget was limited and the chosen building – a concrete high-bay warehouse shell typical of the region, without windows or any building services – required extensive design intervention to make it fit for purpose.

The scheme included the insertion of a 2,700 square metre (30,000 square foot) mezzanine to create an upper level for executive and administrative staff, plus the addition of all systems, including roof fillers to provide daylighting to the design studios. But what really makes the transformation complete is a 'killer' lobby – a space for fashion shows and informal employee interaction.

The 'boardwalk' leads off from this arena, and the building's various spaces are organized around this primary circulation device as a series of smaller-scale neighbourhoods. Where the boardwalk meets secondary boulevards, icon towers mark breakout spaces. Despite the open environment, new product designs are protected from prying eyes in team areas known as 'design pits'.

In keeping with the boarding theme, this is a project that always maintains a sense of balance while capturing the Quiksilver 'vibe'. **location** Newport Beach, California, USA **client** Quiksilver **completed** 2000 **total floor space** 10,120 square metres (110,000 square feet) **staff** 300

1 View of the main lobby, which reflects Quiksilver's youth-oriented board-riding culture. This social space encourages the type of spontaneity that is integral to the brand image

2

2 A translucent tower made of aluminium and sandblasted glass with birch ply panels suggests a 'beach structure'. It houses a lounge enclosure and a double-height office

3 Sandblasted glass panels front mezzanine level executive offices. The Quiksilver brand is visible throughout the environment

4 View of the polished concrete 'boardwalk' that bisects the building and forms its primary circulation route. Interconnected showrooms have gridded frontages of transparent and translucent glass

5 Floor plans show the spatial arrangement of the main floor (left) and the mezzanine

3

4

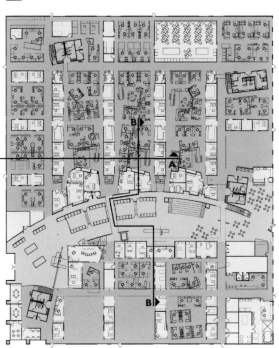
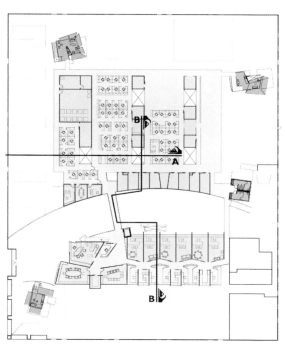

5

FOLLOWING PAGES
6, 7
Interior views show how the Quiksilver scheme plays with honest, low-tech materials to create imaginative compositions in keeping with the beachfront theme

narrative: Quiksilver

**Sony
London, UK
Fletcher Priest Architects**

SONY Playstation has become one of the world's most powerful brands. So it is not surprising that the European headquarters responsible for Playstation's global marketing and sales activity in more than 90 countries should subtly reflect in the interior's colour, form and details the spirit and dynamism of its popular computer games. Welcome, in effect, to Lara Croft's secret hideout – or the Tomb Raider's tomb.

Architects Fletcher Priest started with unpromising material: seven floors of a standard new-build speculative office block in London's Soho district. But the design team rewrote the script completely, introducing the play on Playstation immediately on entry to a flexible double-height reception space at ground-floor level. Formerly a marble-clad corporate lobby, this now has a timber floor that folds upwards to wrap the lift core, forming a screen through which there are external views of Golden Square. Another wall clad in translucent panels wraps around the reception desk and a ground-floor meeting room is suspended unexpectedly in space. Virtual-reality gaming characteristics are simulated in interior space.

At lower-ground-floor level, a spectacular multi-use space has been created with facilities (including an all-weather garden) for launches and conferences that can accommodate up to 250 visitors. The five upper floors are meanwhile given over to efficient office space, but the spirit of Sony Playstation permeates the entire environment.

A special budget was created so that the familiar symbols on the Playstation handset – cross, triangle, square and circle – could be echoed throughout the building. Some applications are clearly stated – in furniture and level signage, for example. Others are to be found in more secret and unexpected places such as courtyard planters and drain covers. This is a scheme that plays with the secret codes and hidden levels inherent in the Playstation brand in a richly inventive way, giving Sony an office that is serious fun.

location London, UK **client** Sony Computer Entertainment Europe **completed** October 2000 **total floor space** 2,930 square metres (31,550 square feet) **staff** 200

1 Playstation's fantasy world is simulated in the generous reception area. The light-suffused Perspex desk and walls change colour and intensity. The wooden flooring folds dynamically upwards. The shape of the furniture has echoes of a hand console

1

2

2 View of the flexible
multi-use space on
the lower ground
floor, which has five
meeting rooms that
can be folded back
for major events

3 Interior view of the
café space. Above
are the white beech
timber boards of
the cantilevered
boardroom

4 Cross section of
the cantilevered
boardroom

5 Floor plan of the
sixth-floor offices

6 Plans for the ground
floor (above) and
lower ground floor
present a generous
landscape of fantasy
and imagination

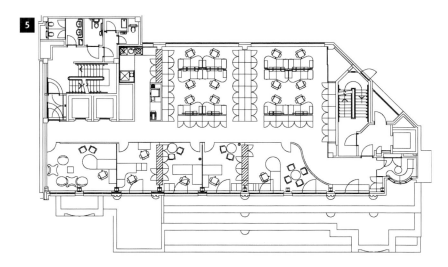

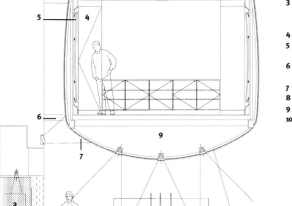

key
1. air-conditioning duct
2. speakers
3. stretched-fabric suspended ceiling with lights behind
4. equipment cupboard
5. curved wall with slots for acoustic absorption
6. bridge with ground-glass surface
7. white beech board
8. café servery
9. plenum
10. pool table

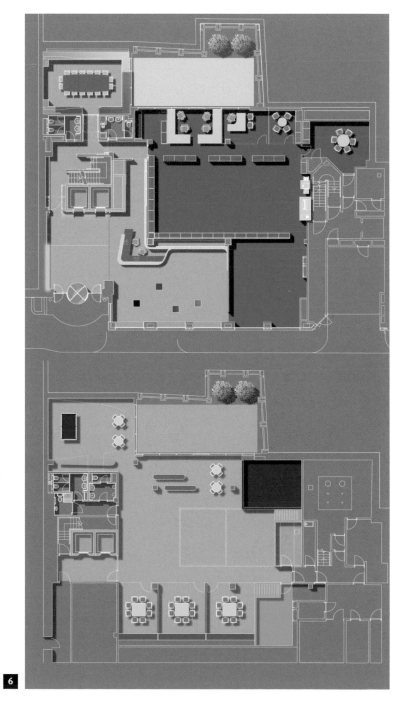

narrative: Sony

Ogilvy & Mather
Los Angeles, USA
Shubin + Donaldson Architects

28 WHEN venerable advertising firm Ogilvy & Mather decided to quit its traditional office in a west Los Angeles corporate tower, it was looking not just for a new place to work but for a new way to work. The agency, founded by the charismatic David Ogilvy and today part of the global WPP Group, wanted to shed its rather staid Madison Avenue-style image in favour of a more open, democratic and creative approach in which old hierarchies would be broken down.

This explains the choice of new location in an Eric Owen Moss building at Culver City – a modern development with an expansive glazed façade incorporating the entrance portals and high ceilings topped with exposed timber – and the appointment of hip young architects Russell Shubin and Robin Donaldson to fit out the 2,800 square metre (30,000 square foot) open-plan floor.

Given such a distinctive architectural shell, the designers faced a challenge to impose their own authority on the interior. Their idea was to avoid explicit city-planning metaphors seen elsewhere in ad agency offices in California and express Ogilvy & Mather's communal workstyle in a looser, more casual way. The scheme's narrative element is set up on entry to Moss's building with a perforated metal 'time tunnel', 13.4 metres (44 feet) long and lined with LCD monitors showing agency showreels, which takes visitors on a journey to the heart of the firm.

The project concentrates the workforce in the front portion of the building with facilities for client interaction in the rear, but in truth the entire scheme plays with notions of translucency and transparency. The time tunnel leads into a main work area of custom-designed desking, with ancillary features such as a library, production area and listening rooms zoned off by giant acrylic panels.

The industrial metaphors and the use of the framed words of the company's founder to remind people why they are at work – 'We sell or get fired' – could make the scheme appear brutal. But, in the same way as the raw-concrete floor is interrupted by carpeting to soften the factory effect, so the project as a whole balances authority with a lightness of touch to give Ogilvy & Mather a dynamic new image.

location Los Angeles, USA
client Ogilvy & Mather
completed 2000 **total floor space** 2,800 square metres (30,000 square feet) **staff** 140

1 A night view of the Eric Owen Moss building reveals the interior narrative set up by Ogilvy & Mather in the light industrial space

2 'The Tube' dominates the entrance and creates a powerful route to the rest of the agency. Showreels are screened along the 'journey' to give a heightened experience for staff and visitors alike

"We sell
or else."
1957

"We sell or
get fired."
1997

3 Under a roof of exposed beams, Ogilvy & Mather staff are constantly exposed to the agency's mission to improve its clients' businesses

4 Floor plan

5 Plan of The Tube, which is prefaced by David Ogilvy's signature and clad in perforated metal panels

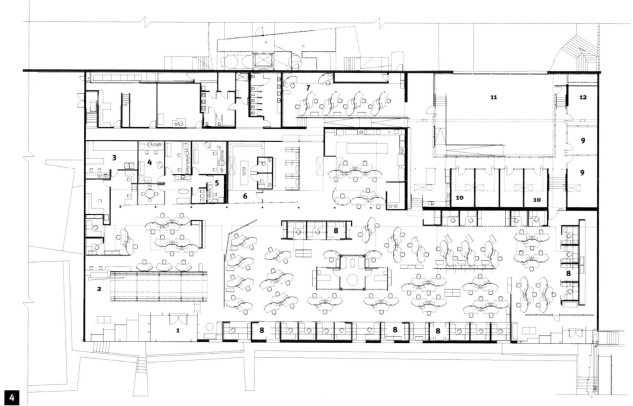

4

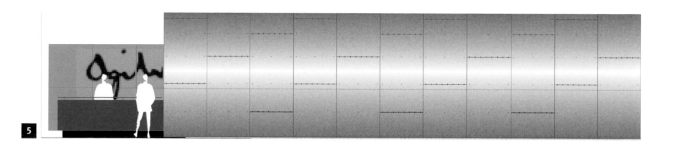

5

narrative: Ogilvy & Mather

6

7

6 Workstations are custom-designed, comprising perforated metal dividers, wood-laminate work surfaces, steel shelves and height-adjustable tables. In a scheme exploring notions of lightness, openness and transparency, these elements are intended to have a solid feel

7 The audio-visual library is clad with acrylic panels

8 The 550 square metre (6,000 square foot) stage pit was developed with Eric Owen Moss. Originally intended for theatrical productions, it has been transformed into a gathering and conference space, flanked by adjacent project rooms

8

Vitra
Weil am Rhein, Germany
Sevil Peach Gence Associates

GERMAN furniture manufacturer Vitra wanted to 'live and breathe' its famous products and brands when it decided to refurbish a part of its renowned Nicholas Grimshaw-designed factory building on a site that is also home to the Vitra Design Museum. Given Vitra's 'work spirit' philosophy and strong design heritage, there was a need to be both bold and representative.

Designer Sevil Peach set out to create a series of settings that demarcate zones based on specific function or workstyle within the open-plan space. Having stripped back the building to its slab, innovations such as movable panels that hang from concrete beams were introduced to divide the large interior into team areas and provide an acoustic baffle and projection surface.

Some owned or assigned workstations are provided alongside a series of 'non-territorial' settings; these are interspersed with communication zones that include a café, breakout area, group rooms and meeting spaces. The concept plan shows key areas defined as either 'team' or 'project', with areas for collaboration in between as well as facilities such as the library and archive.

Two wooden-floored 'patios' introduce light, air and greenery into a space with little natural light. Around these two anchors are a series of zones designed for different activities. Centralized areas for copying and printing are located alongside a main bank of US-style mailboxes; these are used for incoming and outgoing mail and are strategically placed next to the café to encourage interaction and reinforce the circulation routes. A 'caravan and pick' area is also provided as a place for storage of possessions and office equipment.

The workplace uses a cordless internal phone system to allow people to work and be contacted anywhere, and provision is made for nomadic laptop users. But while technology is a key enabler, the overriding impression is of a scheme that represents Vitra's values and provides a showcase for its furniture by such star designers such as Eames, Citterio and Arad. This is a workplace that challenges the rules, anticipating office life in the 21st century and attaching Vitra's name to it. **location** Weil am Rhein, Germany **client** Vitra **completed** 1998 **total floor space** 2,250 square metres (24,220 square feet) **staff** 120

1 A scribble board at reception gives a friendly welcome

2, 3
The heart of the Vitra office is a 'main street' complete with a US-style mailbox for each employee. Staff 'live' the brand, using Vitra designer furniture from Charles Eames to Ron Arad

4

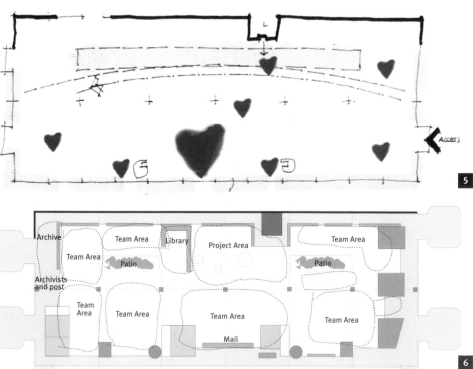

5

6

4 A wooden-floored 'patio' adjacent to a quiet room and library introduces light and air into the work environment, creating a domestic oasis. This semi-enclosed setting helps to 'anchor' an open workplace

5, 6 Concept plans for the project showing hubs for collaboration (the hearts) and zones that demarcate team and ancillary areas

7 Floor plan showing mix of workplace settings. Future office trends are explored and represented through use of Vitra products via a careful orchestration of thinking cells, touchdown zones, project rooms, territorial and non-territorial workspaces, 'patios' and meeting areas

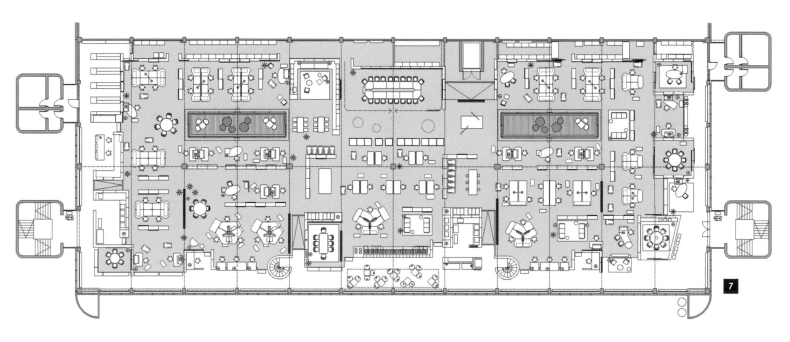

narrative: Vitra

8

8 View of pool table
and 'patio' across
open-plan work area

9 Verner Panton furniture,
a classic in the Vitra
catalogue, provides
an unusual breakout
space for staff

10 In its domestic touches,
the Vitra environment
reflects human desire
for office space
that is uncluttered
and unmechanized

11 A giant meeting table
dominates the project
zone for presentations
and large team sessions

Muzak
Fort Mill, South Carolina, USA
Pentagram/Little & Associates

40 MUZAK is the famous name behind the background music heard in elevators, lobbies and shopping malls. As part of the company's shift of identity from a schmaltzy, much-derided technical resource to a much more hip content provider, with 'audio architects' designing complete music systems for clients such as Gap and Microsoft, Muzak decided to move from its Seattle base to a new corporate headquarters closer to the majority of its customers.

Its new facility at Fort Mill, close to the Charlotte metropolitan area in North Carolina, is the result of a collaboration between Pentagram's New York office and Charlotte-based architects Little & Associates. 'Muzak City' concentrates employees previously scattered around locations in several different cities on one site, as well as housing the world's largest digitized music library.

Space is organized on an urban street grid and occupies a single floor of a warehouse-style building. The environment is totally open and the CEO shares the same workspace as the newest employee. Sound studios have glass doors so the work process is transparent throughout the organization. Public and circulation spaces hug the perimeter of the building so that all can share external views.

Muzak's many private meeting rooms are sited at 'street' intersections, styled as solid buildings within the 'city' and lit by skylights. Each has a different material treatment – wood, cork, metal, masonry – to create local, easily recognizable landmarks in the office. As befits a company that has reinvented itself in recent years, the new circular Muzak identity by Pentagram is repeated throughout the interior in such details as round panel cutouts in reception. And, yes, music does pump through the building at all times. This is a company that really lives the brand.

location Fort Mill, South Carolina, USA **client** Muzak **completed** October 2000 **total floor space** 9,200 square metres (100,000 square feet) **staff** 350

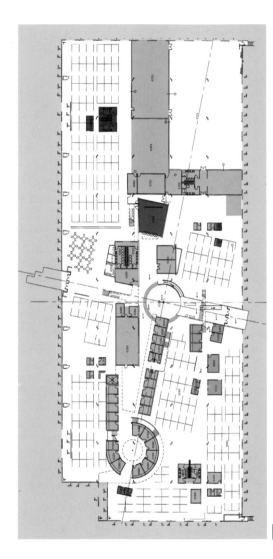

1 Muzak's new circular corporate identity is a repeating motif in the office interior

2 Muzak City's floor plan is based on the idea of an urban grid. Meeting rooms are located at 'street' intersections

3 The reception area presents a strong branded design statement

4

5

6

4 Muzak's 'city centre'
  provides a gathering
  space for all employees

5 As an expression of
  corporate democracy,
  open-plan workstations
  are the same for
  everyone

6 Muzak's audio
  architects work in
  their own rotunda
  in a series of
  enclosed spaces

narrative: Muzak

**Issey Miyake
Tokyo, Japan
Kajima Design**

44 JAPANESE fashion designer Issey Miyake enjoys such a worldwide reputation for innovative form, bold colour and unique texture that it is something of a shock to discover that his new headquarters is not based in a custom-designed architectural masterpiece. Instead, the company has rented space in a large, speculative office building designed and built by Kajima for a developer, the Itochu Corporation.

However, closer inspection reveals that each of the six floors of the Tokyo office block offers large, comfortable, column-free workspace that is an ideal neutral canvas for the Issey Miyake brand to work its magic. On an irregularly shaped site, each floor occupies a rectilinear area of approximately 25 x 18 metres (82 x 59 feet) with multi-purpose areas and service elements such as stairs, elevators and rest rooms integrated into the plan to fit irregular leftover spaces.

A generous 3.6 metre (12 foot) ceiling height is achieved with the help of underfloor air conditioning and a special built-in artificial lighting system. Natural light penetrates the building through a glass curtain wall façade which faces onto Tokyo's Yoyogi Koen Park, affording staff expansive views of rich greenery within a dense urban context.

A hangar-like presentation hall is sited in the building's large basement; on the floors above, the workspace is laid out using mainly rectilinear forms that mirror the floorplates. The overall effect is creamy, calming and spacious, with the only flashes of colour provided by Issey Miyake fabrics and designs.

This is a scheme that does not so much choreograph a journey through a corporate headquarters as simply present the brand philosophy as space to invent.

location Tokyo, Japan **client** Itochu Corporation **completed** 2000 **total floor space** 5,408 square metres (58,210 square feet)

1 This speculative office block in Tokyo is an unlikely setting for one of the world's greatest fashion designers

2 The Issey Miyake headquarters presents a neutral white canvas against which the fashion fabrics and clothing stand out

narrative: Issey Miyake

3

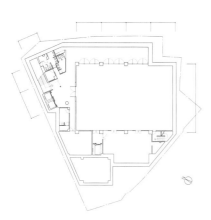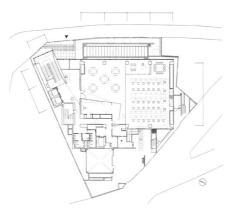

4

5

3 Work areas have
unusually high
ceilings for a
speculative office.
A custom lighting
system integral
to the ceiling leaves
overhead vistas
uncluttered

4 Floor plans showing
(from left) basement,
ground-floor and
third-floor layouts

5 The basement
presentation hall
creates a generous
fashion gallery

6 Private meeting
room with a view
of the greenery
in a Tokyo park

6

narrative: Issey Miyake

DZ Bank
Berlin, Germany
Gehry Partners

48 A STONE'S throw away from the historic Brandenburg Gate in Berlin is a workplace that contains one of master architect Frank Gehry's most powerfully sculptural pieces of work. Not that you would know it from the outside. The planning restrictions that dictate that all new development in the area should refer politely to the gate, built in 1788, meant that Gehry was never going to do a Bilbao Guggenheim number in the new capital of Germany even if he had wanted to.

Instead Gehry's big branch office scheme for DZ Bank, a Frankfurt-based financial services company, hides its awesome sculptural secret away behind the discreet façade of a well-mannered modern building that provides 17,500 square metres (190,000 square feet) of office space as well as 39 apartments on the south flank of a sober mixed-use project.

That interior secret is a breathtaking object shaped, according to Gehry, like the skull of a fossilized prehistoric horse's head. Sited in the building's giant skylit central atrium with offices around the perimeter on three sides, the 'skull' is at once inspiring and menacing, and it encloses within its fantastical form a unique womb-like conference room lined with strips of red oak.

Gehry's signature sinuousness, unfurling itself beneath a delicate lattice of glass and steel, is deliberately at odds with the rational plainness of the exterior. But this is a scheme of many surprises. Beneath the conference chamber, a scooped-out basement level contains a lecture theatre, café and foyer, itself enclosed by a warped-glass canopy that mimics the atrium roof.

Critics have questioned why Gehry should deploy such powerful symbolism for such a prosaic end. A commercial interior is hardly a cultural landmark in the same way that a public gallery might be. Berlin is also a difficult place to advertise such dark, brooding, skull-like imagery that plays on the subconscious (Albert Speer's bunker was found during excavations of the site). But there is no doubt that DZ Bank has been given a new identity based on wielding a monumental aesthetic power, and all staff have a view of it from wherever they work in the building. **location** Berlin, Germany **client** DZ Bank **completed** May 2001 **total floor space** 20,000 square metres (215,300 square feet) **staff** 150

1 Sober, rational frontage is in line with planning restrictions which favour well-mannered elegance over flamboyant gesture

2 The DZ Bank's skylit central atrium reveals its shocking and spectacular secret. A sculptural meeting room shaped like a prehistoric horse's head is delicately suspended between glass canopies above and below

3 A grid of wood-framed perimeter offices have a view of the horse's head structure in the atrium, setting up a tension between the straight-lined and the sinuous

4 Glass-roofed reception area beneath the belly of the beast is hung with glass sculptures by Nikolaus Weinstein

4

3

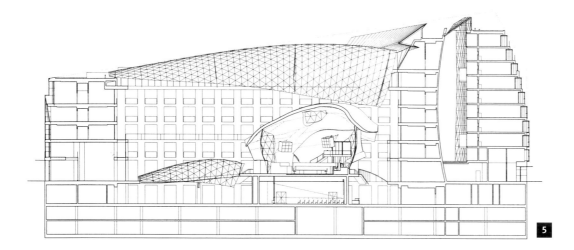

5

5 Longtitudinal section shows the beast-like conference room caged within the formal geometry of the building

6 Cross sections

7 Ground-floor plan showing atrium framed by perimeter offices with access to natural light, in keeping with regulations

8 Inside the conference chamber. Perforated strips of wood create a warm, womb-like space. Any sense of menace is external

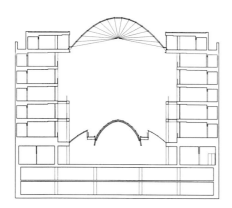

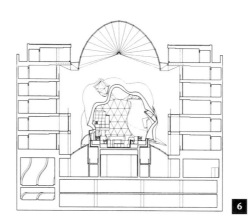

6

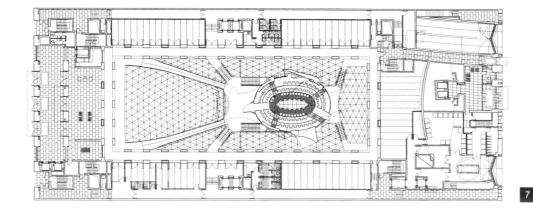

7

8

Duffy
New York City, USA
MAP

54 DUFFY Design is a leading US specialist in creating brand identities, so it is not surprising that the Minneapolis-based firm should take great care to project the right image through its New York office. Duffy's skilfully constructed narrative, designed on one floor of the landmark Woolworth Building in Manhattan, is of the creative command centre with explicit references to sci-fi movies and pioneer modernism.

The futuristic look begins with a circular reception area and desk – and the use of contemporary organic form extends throughout the interior. Orange and light blue are the accent colours on bright white walls. Integral to the scheme is a gallery corridor with curved walls offering inset display areas and a video screen showing recent work. This leads into the main work area, which consists of three groups of eight workstations connected by circular portals that allow sight-and-sound communication along the length of the office.

Running alongside this arrangement, just across a narrow corridor, is a sequence of small meeting and telephone privacy rooms. These have clear-glass floor-to-ceiling windows and sliding doors onto the work areas and floor-to-ceiling glazing to the exterior of the building, enabling natural light to penetrate to the heart of the scheme.

Duffy Design prides itself on teamwork, so the space-crew analogy of the New York office is a fitting one. Indeed the firm was an active collaborator with the architect MAP in developing the new interior, although only one-third of a prepared scheme of 1,840 square metres (20,000 square feet) was actually fitted out. The project, which also includes larger presentation rooms, a kitchen and a dining room, creates a high-tech place to work that is exciting and calming at the same time.

location New York City, USA **client** Duffy Design **completed** 2000 **total floor space** 610 square metres (6,600 square feet) **staff** 30

1 The contemporary curves of the reception desk set the tone for an interior with a strong emphasis on organic forms

2 View into meeting room: the design of the environment has a futuristic sci-fi theme

3 The main work area is a series of interlinked spaces glimpsed through giant, open portholes

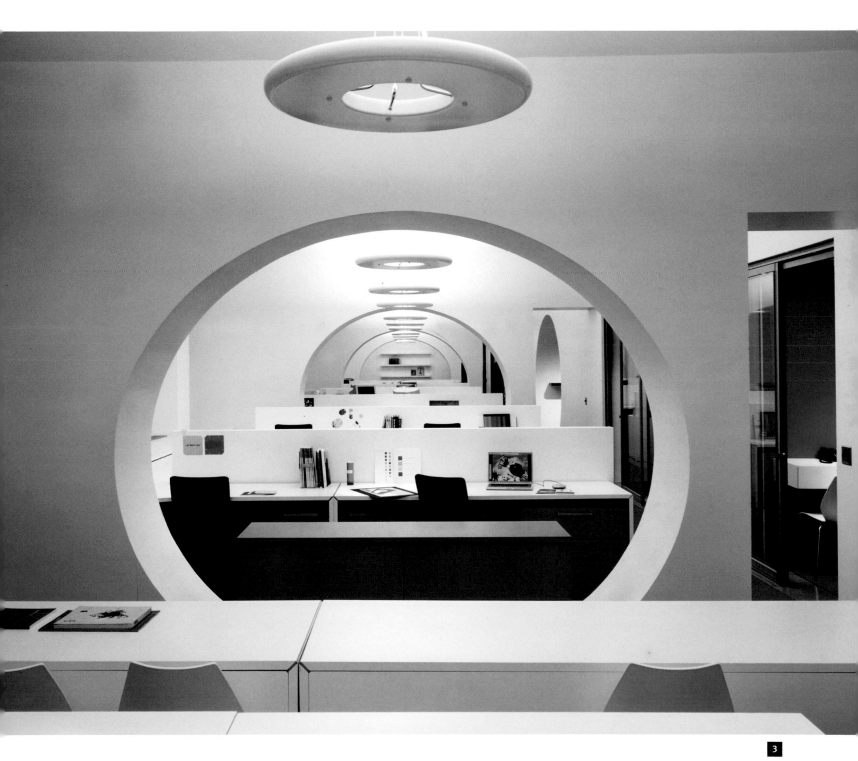

3

Bloomberg
London, UK
Powell-Tuck Associates

56

MOVEMENT, colour and communication lie at the heart of this European headquarters project, which is a visual commentary on Bloomberg as a major provider of news, data and analysis on financial markets around the world. But the challenge facing designers Powell-Tuck Associates was not simply to bring a single office alive but to link and animate two separate buildings in order to create a dynamic, unified work environment reflecting the brand values of a fast-moving global media organization.

By early 2000, Bloomberg's rapid growth was such that refurbishment of its London base at City Gate House in Finsbury Square no longer provided enough accommodation. (City Gate House had been designed in the 1920s as a 'gentlemen's club' by F.R. Gould and Giles Gilbert Scott, architect of the Bankside Power Station.) Next door was a speculative office building designed by Sir Norman Foster. When Bloomberg acquired the lease to the Foster building, its design brief was to link the neighbours physically. City Gate House was to be retained as the main entrance; one catering facility was to serve both buildings.

The key to the project was in relocating the reception and a 'Pantry' serving food and drink from the ground floor to the first floor of City Gate House, so bringing a social 'hub' closer to the physical centre of the combined buildings and expanding it into the links that open up the two separate sites into one. Staff and visitors reach the first-floor reception via two dramatic glass-sided escalators from a darkened entrance lobby which screens Bloomberg services high on glazed walls.

After the dark intensity of the lobby, the Pantry is light and airy, the meeting point for the Bloomberg 'family'. Food is laid out on six glowing white servery drums. Alongside the Pantry, atrium links reveal the way the scheme slices into the Foster building next door, opening up vistas for movement and people-watching. Other aspects of the scheme include a 320-seat auditorium, art spaces, informal breakout areas, meeting rooms and a series of illuminated glazed screens that extend up through the building.

Each office floor has its own signature colour applied to screens, carpets and a perimeter lighting feature, and every employee has a standard Knoll Hannah desk in open-plan space. There are no executive suites or management enclaves. This is a democratic project in which the static workstations provide a counterpoint to the constant flow of people through the imaginative shared facilities and links that animate and electrify the two buildings.

location London, UK **client** Bloomberg **completed** September 2001 **total office space** 13,695 square metres (147,410 square feet) **staff** 2,000

1 View from top of entrance escalators into the Pantry. The darkened lobby below has a hidden camera that transfers the silhouette of people passing through onto a LED (light emitting diode) light frieze

narrative: Bloomberg

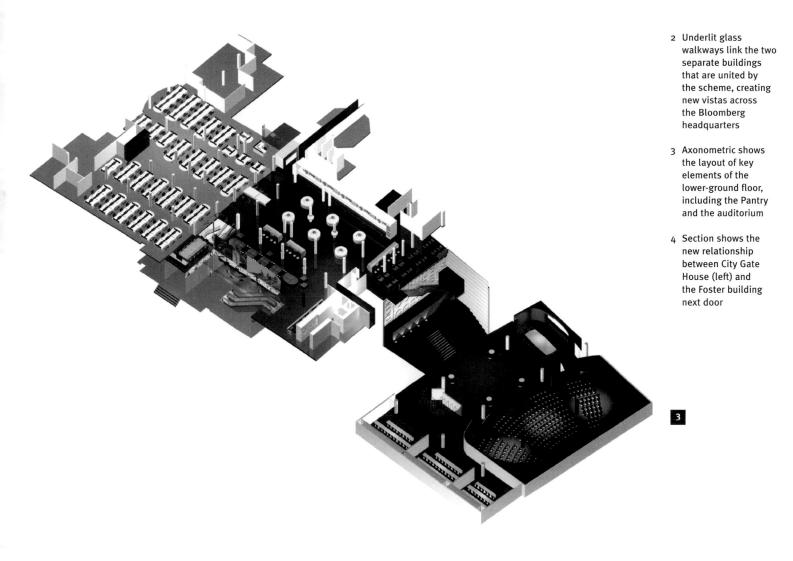

2 Underlit glass walkways link the two separate buildings that are united by the scheme, creating new vistas across the Bloomberg headquarters

3 Axonometric shows the layout of key elements of the lower-ground floor, including the Pantry and the auditorium

4 Section shows the new relationship between City Gate House (left) and the Foster building next door

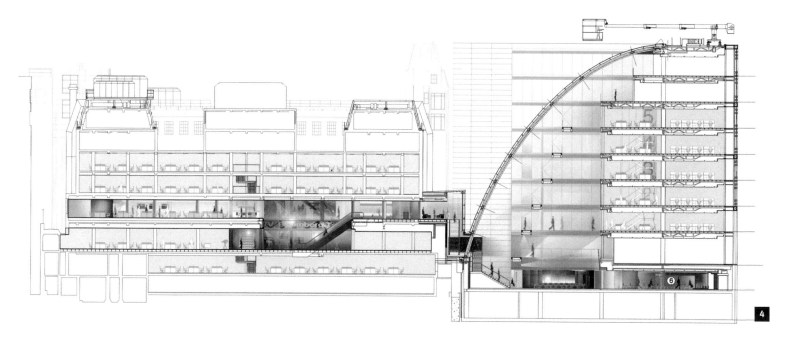

narrative: Bloomberg

5

5 Glass-boxed meeting
rooms maintain a
sense of openness
and transparency
while offering
confidentiality

6 Inside the Pantry,
food is laid out on
white servery drums

7 Coloured lighting
effects define each
office level and add
a sense of dynamism
to the interior.
Bloomberg journalists
are often filmed in
their own space

8 Curated art spaces
such as this bed
of flowers break up
the technological
uniformity of
the media-driven
Bloomberg office

6

7

8

Oliva-Remolà
Barcelona, Spain
Amadeu Oliva i Uriel

62

THIS office for a Spanish architect is located in a rundown industrial suburb of Barcelona. It is surrounded by undistinguished residential property in the crowded Terrassa district. But despite the low-grade environment and the constraints of a very narrow site, this studio building is a real jewel slotted neatly into the dense urban context, providing an excellent work environment and creating a visible advertisement for the architect's services.

The scheme cleverly exploits a difference in level of nearly 5 metres (19 feet) between the street at the front and the street at the rear of the building. At the front, the studio has five storeys that look onto a new park. The building is entered through a perforated-metal sheet door that provides views of a ground-floor gallery even when shut; the four levels above the gallery are open-plan and glass-fronted.

The rear of the building looks onto a semi-pedestrian street and adopts a different strategy, presenting a more opaque façade on three levels. Uniting both sides of the ultra-slim studio – which is just 3.9 metres (13 feet) wide but 24 metres (79 feet) in height – is a lift and stairwell that act as the backbone of the building, articulating and unifying its interior spaces. The use of glass dividers and a white staircase creates an interior journey up to a wood-lined rooftop terrace offering wide vistas across the city.

This project makes the best of a tight site. It uses a simple and consistent palette of concrete, glass, wood and metal to create a tall, thin building that seems to suggest architectural aspiration in its external form and in the interior narrative that form sets up. **location** Barcelona, Spain **client** Oliva-Remolà Architecture **completed** March 1999 **total floor space** 319.68 square metres (3,441 square feet) **staff** 6

1 Rear façade of the ultra-slim studio has three storeys to match a higher street level than at the front

2 Front façade presents five storeys looking onto a park: a near-perfect architectural advertisement for fitting a useful building into an awkward site

3 Staircase unifies the scheme's interior spaces

1

2 3

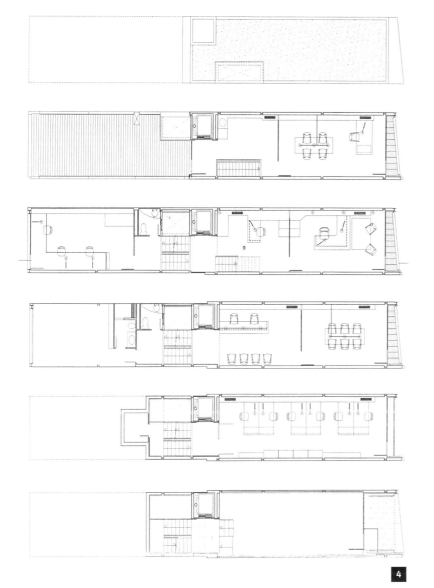

4

4 Floor plans show
   the layout of the five
   levels plus the roof
   terrace

5 Work areas are set
   off the staircase

6 At the top of the stairs
   the journey ends at a
   rooftop terrace

5

6

Reebok
Canton, Massachusetts, USA
NBBJ

66 CAN a new corporate office help to revitalize a brand and completely refocus a company? Sportswear giant Reebok certainly thinks so after investing US $70 million in a spectacular new global headquarters 24 kilometres (15 miles) south of Boston. The manufacturer famed for its culture of athleticism suffered a dip in performance in the late 1990s. Its market share diminished and it badly needed to recover the inspirational spark and energy that had first fired the Reebok name to success.

A project to develop a new headquarters building, uniting on one campus 1,000 employees scattered across five sites, became an exercise in corporate renewal. On an 18 hectare (44 acre) rural site, designers NBBJ proposed a singular, sleek structure formed around a curving transparent glass spine and surrounded by seven athletics fields and activity areas. Angled off the spine are three four-storey office wings and an executive block including a 1,380 square metre (15,000 square foot) conference centre.

The overall plan has the coiled energy of an athlete on the starting blocks. Indeed, what is so distinctive about the Reebok project is the way sports and fitness facilities are woven inside and outside the building.

Product testing is a big part of the Reebok culture and there is ample opportunity to get the suit off here. Nature, daylight, fresh air and physical activity – themes traditionally alien to office design – are integral to this project.

From the spine, there are views onto an indoor basketball court and into a glass tunnel that takes a running track into the building from outside. A fitness centre, café and shop are dispersed along the spine to promote interaction in a scheme that emphasizes open circulation throughout. In the office wings, space is open-plan, and high ceilings and a long span structure allow for future planning flexibility.

The environment has by all accounts had a galvanizing effect on the company and its employees, helping to revitalize the brand and introducing a new take on the corporate campus that rethinks the relationship between indoors and outside, work and leisure.

location Canton, Massachusetts, USA
client Reebok International
completed June 2000 **total floor space** 48,020 square metres (522,000 square feet)
staff 1,000

1 Exterior view shows the easy juxtaposition of business and sport in the way the Reebok headquarters is organized. The façade was conceived as a view towards the curved segment of a sports stadium. Outdoor activity is integral to the life of the campus

2 Inside the glass spine there are open views across and between levels

1

2

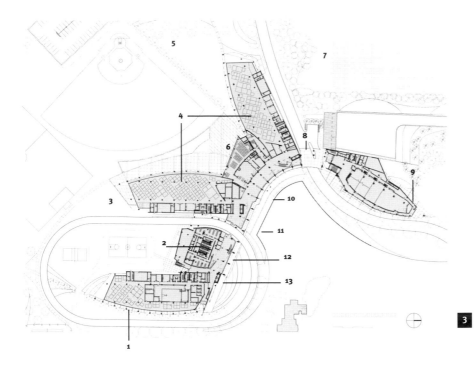

key
1 biomechanical lab
2 fitness area, including
   basketball court
3 tennis courts
4 offices
5 soccer field
6 terrace
7 softball field
8 driveway
9 executive offices and
   conference centre
10 visitor entrance
11 glass-enclosed spine
12 running track below
   building
13 café

3

3 The plan of the
  building has the
  coiled energy of an
  athlete waiting
  for the starting gun

4 The building is lifted
  and layered on its site
  to create challenging
  geometries and allow
  for crossover and
  meeting points
  that encourage
  spontaeous social
  interaction

5 Sloping glazed walls
  frame social spaces
  in an environment
  dedicated to living
  the Reebok brand

4

6

6 Slatted, curved
   roofline frames
   two players in the
   Reebok narrative

7 Sports facilities
   are integral to the
   building, rather
   than an add-on

8 Inside a Reebok
   staffer's cellular
   office. Staff are
   encouraged to test
   the product, and the
   sports facilities of
   the new headquarters
   are right at hand to
   help them to do it

7

8

narrative: Reebok

**Fuksas
Rome, Italy
Massimilano and
Doriana Fuksas**

72 AS a leading international architect, Massimilano Fuksas has made a career out of understanding the constant process of change and exploring the tensions between history and modernity. So it is entirely appropriate that his architectural practice Fuksas Associati should site its Rome office (there are also offices in Vienna and Paris) in an updated 16th-century *palazzo* that reveals the layers of different centuries in its curiously worn, rubbed and washed walls.

Fuksas describes his Rome office as the only place in which he can be 'truly creative', and the interior certainly appears tailor-made for his kind of architectural enquiry. Modern additions coexist with the original structure, forming a whole that mirrors Rome itself, which has been described as the 'layered city'. Each interior wall tells its own story with layers of past decor, including mural paintings, deliberately exposed and preserved under wax.

A weathered main stairway leads from an interior courtyard to the entrance lobby, which is divided from a meeting room by a glass partition. A glass lift rises through a timber floor to the second of three floors where the practice architects work in project groups in adaptable open space. Fuksas himself occupies the third floor, with large rooms and high windows.

The architect calls his workplace a 'collage office'. Indeed, there are few fixed points in a largely flexible scheme other than a secretariat, technical core and a model-making room. In this setting, contemporary architectural models hung on the wall assume the same importance as the religious art discovered during the building's many renovations. This is the office as a 'work in progress'. A much-modified *palazzo* is now the subject of Fuksas's attention and affection, and it will surely change again as a reflection of the architect's philosophy.

location Rome, Italy **client** Fuksas Associati **completed** 1998
total floor space 1,000 square metres (10,760 square feet) **staff** 40

1 Glazed elevator in historic conference room exemplifies the engaging juxtaposition of old and new

2 Second-floor plan

3 Main secretarial space in the updated 16th-century *palazzo*. Walls layered with past decor are plastered with a collage of architectural posters

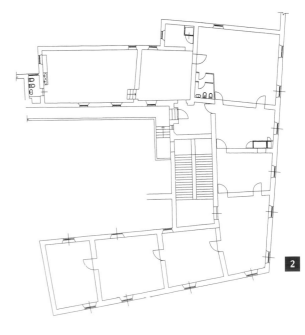

**Allsteel
Muscatine, Iowa, USA
Gensler**

74   THIS project to create a national headquarters for a century-old manufacturer of office furniture transforms a former electrical parts factory in Iowa into a stylish office-cum-showroom. But it does more than just imaginatively recycle an old industrial building – it demonstrates how a new work environment can help a company to establish an independent brand identity.

Allsteel wanted to build a distinctive profile as a separate entity from its parent, HON International. Its target market is design-sensitive architects and specifiers, but its rural Midwestern location ran counter to that aspiration, and its brand was losing value after being tied too closely to the parent company. Gensler's task was to turn Allsteel's Midwestern heritage into a plus point without resorting to cliché, and to re-establish the manufacturer as modern and design-oriented.

The solution lay in translating a homespun Midwestern philosophy of fairness, honesty and integrity into a series of residential metaphors designed to capture the essence of the new brand and communicate it effectively to employees and a large visiting community of furniture installers, specifiers and end users.

The mood is set directly upon entering the building, by a 'community centre' comprising reception, meeting space and café. Armchairs, rocking chairs and a slip-covered sofa are grouped congenially around a fireplace; indeed, the residential furniture used throughout the building's common spaces contrasts well with the contract ranges on offer.

'Honest' materials such as exposed ductwork and concrete floors further convey the no-nonsense appeal of the Allsteel brand, while use of features such as translucent panels suggests a dynamic design approach. The result is not simply an exercise in metropolitan chic; the water towers and farm fields of the surrounding area are interpreted in the interior as abstract, bold forms. A special carpet reflects the local landscape, for example, in a scheme that achieves just the right balance between rural charm and business efficiency. **location** Muscatine, Iowa, USA **client** Allsteel Inc. **completed** November 2000 **total floor space** 6,000 square metres (65,000 square feet) **staff** 131

1   Floor plan reveals a mix of showroom, demonstration area and working space

2   Office as living room: this scheme promotes homespun, Midwestern family values by giving visitors comfortable seats, rockers and a sofa grouped around a fireplace in a social space next to reception

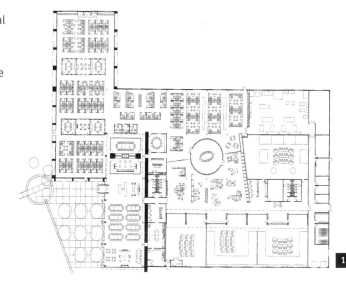

1

3, 4
A palette of 'honest'
materials – exposed
ductwork, concrete
and glass – suggests
the integrity of the
manufacturer while
sending a signal
about contemporary
design

5 A custom-designed
carpet in product-
demonstration
areas derives its
abstract pattern
from an aerial view
of local farmland

narrative: Allsteel

Toyota
Epsom Downs, UK
Sheppard Robson

78 THE new UK headquarters of Japanese car maker Toyota makes explicit visual reference to the automotive industry in its curved forms, crisp metallic finishes and spacious interior vistas. New Toyota models are parked in an airy, light-filled internal street that forms an essential part of the plan. But this is a campus-style building that does much more than simply ape aspects of vehicle styling. It has been designed as a robust and considered response to the twin demands of a brownfield site with commanding views of the outskirts of London and an organizational desire to encourage new workstyles.

The £25 million project exploits a wonderful position at Great Burgh close to Epsom racecourse, setting out an expansive office that gives employees more freedom to move around within the building and a greater variety of places to work. The geometries of three distinct elements generate the design: a rotunda sitting on a concrete plinth acts as reception and the main hub of the building; a glazed internal street performs the function of a spine as it curves off the rotunda down an expanse of 80 metres (260 feet); and four splayed office wings, each two storeys high, emerge from the street.

The whole scheme is set in a landscaped park with pine trees, rolling lawns and a lake in front of the building, giving first-time visitors the impression of a balance between nature and technology. Indeed, the scheme has an environmentally friendly focus on energy efficiency. But the overriding impression is of the company's brand ethos being suffused through a series of cool, grey, technically precise spaces linked by galleries, balconies and staircases and finished in glass and steel. People add the colour as they flow through the curving street, visiting the café, a deli/restaurant and balcony breakout areas in a demonstration of Toyota's 'work freedom' philosophy.

A more traditional approach survives in the office wings, with senior managers opting for cellular space while more junior staff work in well-organized open-plan. But there can be no mistaking the bold and radical instincts that underpin the entire project. These are best expressed in the journey from the rotunda into the street where the Toyota narrative is writ large.
location Epsom Downs, UK **client** Toyota (GB) **completed** July 2001 **total floor space** 14,000 square metres (150,700 square feet) **staff** 500

1 Cross section through the building

2 The new Toyota (GB) headquarters reflects a synergy between product, brand and architecture that extends to cars on display in the curved internal 'street'

FOLLOWING PAGES
3 Exterior view of the rotunda at the hub of the building and the street that curves off it

4 Balcony breakout area in the main public boulevard with social space beneath. A range of work settings support Toyota's 'work freedom' ethos

1

2

narrative: Toyota

the 21st century office

5 View from the mezzanine into the light, airy staff restaurant

6 Ground-floor plan showing four splayed office wings radiating out from an internal street 80 metres (260 feet) in length

7 Naturally ventilated open-plan office area represents a more conventional approach

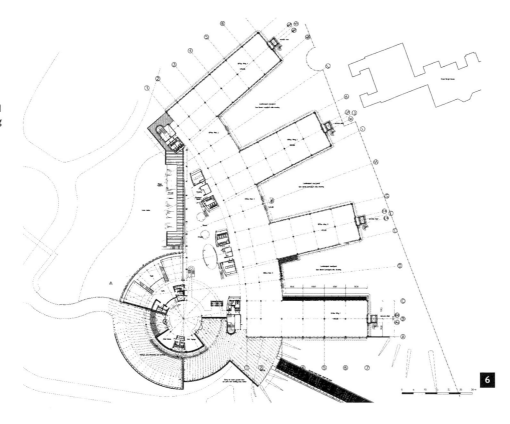

2 nodal

office as knowledge connector

Offices were once planned as fixed architectural containers for work and populated by sedentary workers who rarely shared ideas. But, in the knowledge-driven economy of the 21st century, flexible new offices are emerging that can accommodate unpredictability and enable information to flow more freely because they are nodal in character. The nodal office provides a flexible workforce with a fixed point, a resources centre devoted to coaching, mentoring and fostering the collaborations that lead to successful innovation. In effect, it provides a hub for business – a place to pass through or to connect to from remote places – and it is the physical manifestation of the organization in an increasingly virtual world. This selection of office interiors expresses the nodal theme.

McKinsey & Company
Amsterdam, The Netherlands
Veldhoen + Company

86 THE striking Renzo Piano-designed Nemo Science and Technology Museum in Amsterdam's harbour may seem an unlikely setting for an innovative office for management consultancy McKinsey & Company, but the top floors of the building have been converted to create an unusual and inspirational workplace.

The new office was developed as a place to help clients to set up new e-businesses – a so-called 'incubator space' – as well as to provide a work environment for McKinsey's consultants. The dual purpose created a conceptual challenge for Veldhoen + Company, compounded by the building's unusual form, which includes rounded shapes, slanting walls and ceilings 15 metres (49 feet) high.

The project addresses all these issues with flair. A staircase links the two key floors and provides a natural division between the team rooms downstairs and a combination of more casual work settings and spaces upstairs. Veldhoen had to accommodate different work needs, from collaboration to concentration, as well as variable and fluctuating team sizes. With consultants spending much of their time at clients' sites, and with e-business projects needing teams that might range in size from four to 60 people, flexibility was vital.

Multi-functional team rooms have a consulting table for team meetings as well as single-person workspaces for individual, concentrated work. Cockpits or 'cocoons' allow privacy for individuals, while 'lounges' provide settings where two or three colleagues can work together. Relaxation areas and social spaces complement the more formal work areas. In keeping with Piano's design concept, the architects have kept services exposed and used industrial materials such as steel with exposed rivets and glazed partitioning.

Much of the furniture is custom-designed, including a 'lounge table' that provides a new furniture solution for collaborative work in a semi-private setting. McKinsey consultants all have laptops and mobile phones for constant connectivity. This nodal space provides a rich array of work settings, showing that real flexibility can be achieved for an unpredictable work requirement from both internal and external people.

location Amsterdam, The Netherlands **client** McKinsey & Company **completed** 2000 **total floor space** 900 square metres (9,700 square feet) **staff** 110

1 The Nemo Science and Technology Museum in Amsterdam is home to this nodal workspace for McKinsey, which is located at the top of the building

2 Workers use purpose-designed 'lounge tables' for individual work or collaboration. Electronic controls make tables and bench seats fully adjustable, and power and data are delivered to the table surfaces

1

nodal: McKinsey & Company

3 Lounge tables in
   semi-enclosed spaces
   encourage chance
   meetings. In the
   centre of the floor
   is a servery counter
   and refreshment
   area that provides a
   focus for this office

4 Plan of main floor
   shows enclosed
   meeting rooms and
   lounge tables as well
   as the central counter

5 Team rooms are
   designed so that
   people working on
   a project can be
   co-located. They
   provide a range of
   facilities in a self-
   contained setting

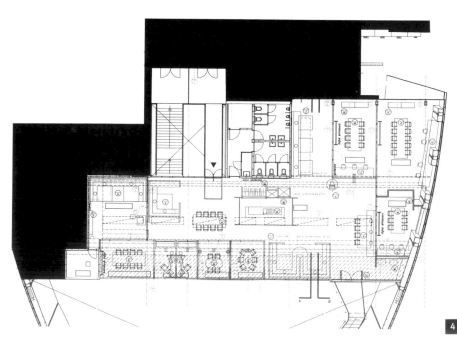

nodal: McKinsey & Company

Winstar
New York City, USA
Graham Hanson Design

90

IN the digital world of invisible bits and bytes, the importance of somewhere to demonstrate products and technologies has ironically become a more central part of workspace function. Such nodal locations often provide the only 'physical' point of contact for customers accessing virtual services – as Winstar, a broadband services company and creator of the well-known office.com software suite, recognized.

Needing a dedicated environment to operate alongside its main offices in midtown Manhattan, Winstar created the e.center, a new concept workspace that would embody its high-tech offer. People using the e.center include not only customers but also strategic partners, employees and members of the financial, media and real-estate communities. As such, the space had to perform a variety of functions – sales, briefing and training – and provide both an effective showcase and a real place for work.

Architect Graham Hanson used a freestanding tunnel 9 metres (30 feet) long to control and draw people into the space. This creates a sense of drama on arrival, and clever use of lighting such as the bands of yellow neon attracts visitors in. As people near the end of the tunnel, a series of light boxes presents images reflecting the company's business, and visitors are then delivered into a space that has been designed with an industrial look with exposed services, metal cladding and concrete.

The environment makes effective use of technology for imagery and communications. Full-colour, high-definition LED matrix panels present complex graphics and live data; plasma screens and video monitors broadcast digital data that can be 'personalized' to relate to individuals as they move through the space. During presentations, engineers manage the experience from the e.center's complex control room, drawing people through the space using lighting and multimedia effects, rather than relying on the usual sedentary presentation.

Anyone using the e.center can plug their laptops into data ports to access email, and telephones are scattered through the space. Many nodal centres are add-ons – the poor relations to the main corporate office. Winstar's e.center provides a well-designed environment that is more of a genuine extension of the company.
location New York City, USA **client** Winstar Communications **completed** 2000 **total floor space** 370 square metres (4,000 square feet)

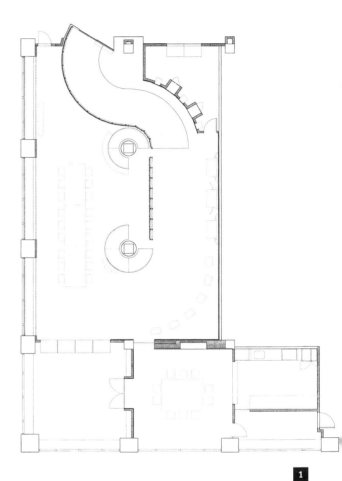

1

1 Floor plan describes a journey through the space, in which people are led down the curved tunnel and into the main presentation zone

2 Glazed partitioning gives the space a translucency, and technology displays such as the LED matrix panels project and reflect messages

2

3 The 9 metre (30 foot) long freestanding tunnel creates a dramatic entrance and provides the journey through the space. Technicians manage the experience with multimedia effects as people move through the environment

3

4 The journey ends in a more formal environment that gives Winstar a forum in which to present its products and services

5 Screens bombard people with imagery and data as they move through the space, and purpose-designed light boxes project pictures that reflect the company's business

4

5

**Valtech
London, UK
Harper Mackay Architects**

96

WHEN Valtech, a global e-business consultancy, moved from cramped offices in London's West End to a new space closer to the City of London, it wanted to create an environment that would facilitate the needs of its nomadic consultants and provide an effective place for training its clients.

Architect Harper Mackay sourced inspiration from Lewis Carroll's *Alice in Wonderland*. Throughout the three-storey office there are intentional juxtapositions and a use of the unexpected to create a sense of adventure and interest. Imaginative graphics – or 'photomurals' – project bold statements and provide drama in a space where contrasts are key. The designers have blended inside and outside by utilizing a decked courtyard as a part of the workspace and introducing visual elements, such as images of a forest, and daylight wherever possible.

Materials also break the mould, with blue corrugated polycarbonate used alongside honeycomb panelling. An orange reception desk running through the wall into the main workspace sets the scene on arrival and builds on the company's visual identity. Throughout the interior there is innovation and surprise, such as the frosted glass used to partition the space that also doubles as a scribble board, and the portable storage units, or 'donkeys', that can be hauled around the space as needed.

Valtech uses the space as both a workplace and a training environment, so good facilities are needed for both nomadic employees and visitors. The space plan itself is innovative, creating a series of unconventionally asymmetrical spaces that articulates a distinctive circulation route through the building. The ground floor provides a nodal zone for consultants to use when they are in the office, with a variety of furniture settings serviced by advanced technology.

Much of the floorplate is given over to social spaces such as a self-service café bar complete with table football, and even a mini-stadium to watch sports events on TV. Technology includes a wireless local area network that allows consultants to 'hot desk' and connect their laptop to the server from anywhere. Laptops can also be connected in a landscaped courtyard, making it an integral part of the office. This project is a good example of a flexible and agile space that provides a stimulating and effective nodal environment for a transitory workforce and a knowledge-hungry customer base.

location London, UK **client** Valtech **completed** 2000 **total floor space** 24,000 square metres (260,000 square feet) **staff** 150

1 Social spaces feature full-height 'photomurals' that introduce natural themes and blur the distinction between indoors and outdoors. Here a forest view gives drama to the café environment

2 Corrugated panelling is used creatively as a partitioning system, and the designer's choice of vibrant blue walls injects colour into the space and hides the training rooms behind

1

2

T1 →
T2 ↗
← T3
← T4

Left hand
"push me
through
the sea"

← Eating area

nodal: Valtech

98

3 Floor plan shows the division of space using angled walls and unorthodox circulation that results in an *Alice in Wonderland* effect

4 Honeycombed panelling is used for walls, and graphics for both signage and branding have also been applied directly to vertical surfaces

5 Exposed services give an industrial feel to the café space, which has Philippe Starck-designed furniture and includes dining tables at which staff can socialize

6 Even the toilet facilities have received special treatment. An Alpine photographic mural provides a dramatic backdrop and builds on the concept of global locations and occurrences

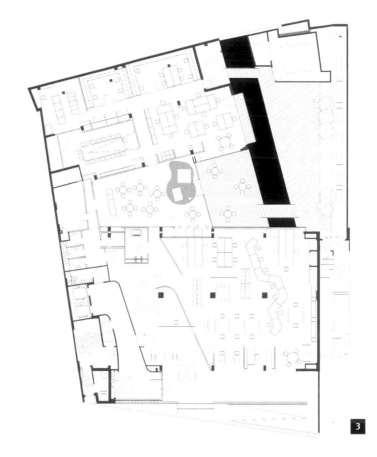

3

4

5

6

PricewaterhouseCoopers
Philadelphia, USA
Gensler

100 THE Zone@PricewaterhouseCoopers is a new workspace concept that enables the firm's technology consultants to educate and interact with client companies, transforming the way they do business. Rather than the flat presentation suite of old with limited capacity for personal interaction, the Zone is a place of contact and learning, where people can come to understand and build a technology solution as 'players' rather than 'spectators' in the development process.

This is a scheme in which physical space plays a key role in knowledge transfer. PricewaterhouseCoopers has brought together demonstration, development and training capabilities in a 'cluster' that provides a place for clients to 'test drive' the process before appointing the consultancy. Light, sound and video effects make a memorable experience for the visitor. Finishes provide a neutral backdrop to the business message, with multimedia technology rather than fixed materials supplying the colour and vibrancy.

There is an Industry Competency Centre where each of the firm's four global practices has its own room designed to reflect the industry it serves: retail and consumer products; energy; information, communications and entertainment; and financial services. A fifth room is reserved for future expansion.

Alongside the competency centre is a development area providing a flexible workspace for consultants that can be quickly reconfigured as required. Although the space accommodates high technology such as interactive white boards and plasma screens, it has also been designed to be 'high touch' and human with use of such materials as leather and wood.

The benefit of such an environment is that it allows clients to eliminate much of the risk and guesswork that can be associated with purchasing technology systems. The space enables consultant and customer to interact and develop a solution together, altering the entire process. In a world of bland product demonstration rooms, architect Gensler has created a setting that is a powerful business differentiator. **location** Philadelphia, USA **client** PricewaterhouseCoopers **completed** 1999 **total floor space** 2,800 square metres (30,000 square feet)

1 Plan of the space shows the zones for presentation and development

2 In the Industry Competency Centre environments are themed to reflect PricewaterhouseCoopers' four key practices

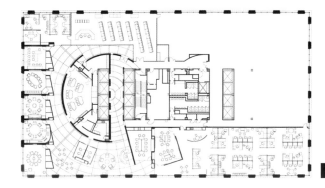

1

3 High technology has been combined with high touch so that the environment is not oppressive. The spaces provide the latest equipment for audio and video, and allow remote conferencing and collaboration

4 A room dedicated to retail and consumer products forms part of the Industry Competency Centre

5 View of lobby. From the outside this building is an unassuming tower in downtown Philadelphia, but inside the space has been transformed into a vibrant centre for this management consultancy

3

4

Oliver, Wyman
New York City, USA
Resolution 4

104 WHEN financial consulting firm Oliver, Wyman set out to create a new headquarters just south of Grand Central Station on Manhattan's Park Avenue, the brief was to develop a welcoming local environment for the company's primarily young, mobile consultants while reflecting the global nature of the firm's business.

The result is a campus-like office for a largely nomadic workforce that is innovative and well considered in design. Banks of 'hot desks' and team settings line the space, and at each end informal lounges are provided for casual meetings and audio conferences. Adjacent to the open-plan areas are ten small private meeting rooms. These are complemented by formal rooms for presentations and video conferencing as well as a number of shared cellular offices for directors.

Jutting into this consultant environment is the 'Zen Zone', a dynamic space meant for impromptu meetings that is articulated by a giant surfboard-like table. Here consultants can touch down, connect their laptops and collaborate with colleagues. On a floorplate where much of the space is open, phone booths provide audio privacy, while the scheme's circulation routes have banks of lockers for people's possessions and equipment.

The one area of permanence, at the centre of the layout, is a work area for support staff based full-time in the office; this group anchors what would otherwise be a transient environment.

A lunch room with a bench-height dining table provides a place for people to socialize, while an information lounge gives consultants knowledge and news. The interior concept plays with shapes and materials to create unusual angles and vistas. Dramatic anodized fins are combined with tensioned fabric, for example, to create an unusual atmosphere.

The club-like environment is ideal for people who need a base where they can drop in or return to. While many nodal offices pay only lip service to anything other than hot desks, Oliver, Wyman has created a series of innovative shared spaces for knowledge, collaboration, communication and relaxation.

location New York City, USA **client** Oliver, Wyman & Co **completed** 2000 **total floor space** 2,800 square metres (30,000 square feet) **staff** 145

1 The Zen Zone is a place for impromptu meetings located in the centre of the floorplate, adjacent to the hot-desk consulting zone. Dominated by a surfboard-like table, it provides a place for collaboration

2 Computer-generated visual shows the structure and layout of the floor

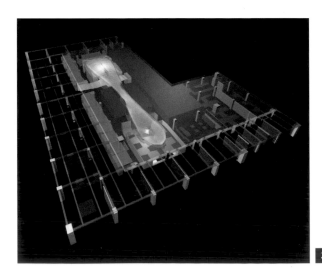

nodal: Oliver, Wyman

3 Meeting rooms in the
centre of the floor are
used for more formal
presentations and
feature imposing
anodized fins and
sandblasted sliding
glass doors

4 Axonometric of the
workstations and
cellular offices,
showing the units
that form banks
of hot desks for
consultants

5 The lunch room where
consultants can relax
and socialize. Shared
dining tables allow
teamwork to continue
over food and drink

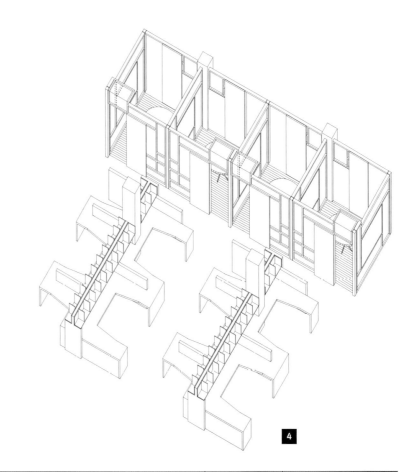

4

3

5

6

6 Circulation space is made
interesting by the use
of sloping walls and the
integration of elements
such as tensioned fabric

7 Primary circulation is
planned at the perimeter,
so that everyone in the
open-plan area shares
what is considered to be
premium space – with
daylight and views

8 To avoid noise pollution in
open-plan from speaker-
phones and to enable
confidential conversations,
phone booths are provided
around the floor

7

8

Media Plaza
Utrecht, The Netherlands
Sander Architekten

110   MEDIA Plaza is a futuristic government information centre in Utrecht whose aim is to make senior decision-makers in Dutch industry more aware of the importance of the information superhighway. Taking managers out of their everyday working lives and encouraging them to stop and think about tomorrow's technologies is achieved in an environment that breaks the rules.

Media Plaza is based in a small hall within the extensive Jaarbeurs trade-fair complex. Given its surroundings, it was essential that the space was different and delivered an 'out-of-this-world' experience. Visitors enter through a giant tube clad with stainless-steel mesh; this leads into a great hall, in which a deliberate sense of movement is achieved by running neon in the flooring and an undulating ceiling.

The original space, opened in 1997, has been renovated and expanded, and the centre can now accommodate 500 people in various settings and zones. The space-age 'highway shuttle' is designed for making presentations to about 20 people, and a series of folding doors gives the impression of ejecting people from the interior into the surrounding spaces after a mission.

A new setting is the 'round control' room; a circular hall in which people are immersed in a total 'image and sound experience' as they 'float by' on chairs. In addition, the media arena is a soundproofed hall that provides seating for 50 people to view multimedia presentations.

Wireless networks allow laptop connection from any of the spaces. The bar and pantry area, for example, has innovative standing-height tables that can be used for work or socializing. There is a series of enclosed rooms and meeting spaces including long tables for laptop-based work or collaborative sessions.

Architect Ellen Sander has created a theatrical space that combines the attributes of a bar and hotel lobby. Media Plaza offers a stimulating and entertaining place for nodal work that embraces the needs of an audience gathering for education and collaboration.
location Utrecht, Holland **client** Media Plaza **completed** November 2000 **total floor space** 3,000 square metres (32,300 square feet)

1 Floor plan showing the original space that has been expanded and refurbished to accommodate an auditorium and new meeting or work rooms

2 Bar and pantry area has standing-height tables that can be used for work or socializing. The environment feels more like an hotel lobby or nightclub than a space for work

FOLLOWING PAGES
3 The 'round control' room is a circular hall in which people are immersed in a total 'image and sound experience'

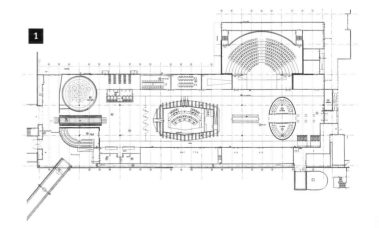

4

4 View into a work
room where people
can connect to the
internet with wireless
laptop computers

5 The sculptural
'highway shuttle',
a presentation zone
for up to 20 people,
forms the nerve
centre of the space

5

IBM
Santa Monica, USA
HOK

116 IBM's e-business office is in effect a cross between a creative studio and a client services, marketing and presentation space. It is here that the skills and knowledge of multi-disciplinary teams are brought together to develop solutions for clients. The way people use the facility has dictated its design, so the scheme provides a team-oriented workplace that incorporates settings for privacy and concentration.

The four-storey building's high ceilings and good natural light are used to advantage by the architect. To encourage interaction, the workspace has both horizontal and vertical circulation, as well as team areas, studio work areas, briefing rooms, touchdown and dining areas. Desking is 'molecular' in layout – a zigzag plan that encourages interaction – and 'hoteling' desks for visitors are provided throughout.

Architect HOK has designed a journey through the space, starting with an immersion presentation on the ground floor that uses technology to get interactive feedback from potential clients (allowing IBM to assess the business prospect in real time). Next stop is the fourth floor, where IBM explains how its people can deliver solutions and tries to close the deal. The third floor is for strategists and creative people who shape the look and feel of the solution, while the second floor is for the technical people who implement the design and create the final product.

The building mirrors the lifecycle of a project from inception to completion and provides an integrated approach that brings the customer into the process. Visitors are segregated in client areas but occupy the space alongside their team. Technology is advanced: the scheme has adopted innovations such as the use of integrated video and projection multimedia with lighting to create programmed 'scenes' that enhance the client's experience.

Aesthetically, the space uses degrees of whiteness – many of the finishes and materials are specified in white, including the flooring. These hard surfaces are complemented by natural maplewood furniture.

As a space designed around the needs of a company, this is a good example of a workplace that fits a process. It represents a trend whereby the client becomes an integral part of the work environment and is encouraged to slot into a nodal workplace to participate in the development process.
location Santa Monica, California, USA **client** IBM
completed 2000 **total floor space** 4,800 square metres
(52,000 square feet) **staff** 200

1 The environment combines creative studio workspace with state-of-the-art client services, marketing and presentation areas

1

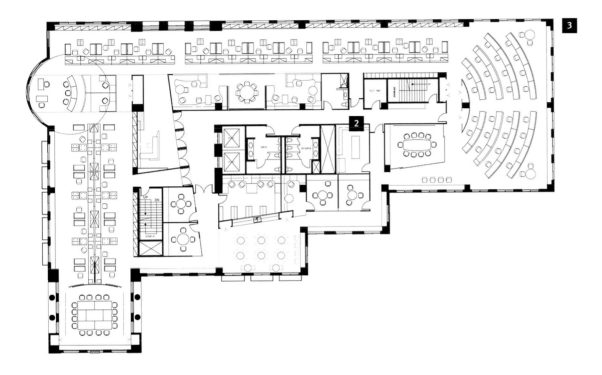

2 The design provides
a white and therefore
neutral backdrop for
the Innovation Centre,
using warm natural
wood tones in floor
and furniture to
project a comfortable,
secure feeling

3 Plan of the third floor,
where strategists and
designers create the
look and feel of the
e-business solution.
The desk layout
encourages teamwork
and interaction

4 Frosted backlit acrylic
panes illuminate
briefing rooms and
can also be used as a
surface for scribbling
notes or diagrams

**RealNames
San Francisco, USA
Blauel Architects**

120 THE dramatic growth of the internet in the late 1990s led to two office-building projects undertaken in close succession for a fast-growing US West Coast technology company, at San Carlos and Red Wood Shores, both near San Francisco. RealNames emerged as a leader in technology for internet keyword navigation until its early demise. Its primarily young, dynamic workforce needed a state-of-the-art workplace to reflect its high-tech drive and accommodate its unpredictable rate of growth.

The initial scheme for 150 people introduced an interesting furniture solution based on 'spines' configured at varying angles to provide an innovative range of workstations. These spines carry the voice, data and power cabling along the length of the building, fed from above by power poles. Ducts and joists are all exposed, and the ceiling has been left in its raw state, giving the office an industrial feel.

Complementing the open areas is a range of meeting spaces housed in transparent fibreglass-panelled rooms. Here lighting has been designed for dramatic effect, casting shadows when meetings take place to indicate that the room is in use. The small pod-shaped meeting rooms are interspersed between the spines and break the monotony of the space. Other facilities for staff include a large leisure area and a café. Since technology is at the heart of the business, the servers on which it relies are exposed and brought into the workplace in a central showcase just off reception, rather than being hidden away in basement rooms.

The second building, for 300 people, was completed a year later. It takes the original concept further, making use of a double-height warehouse space to create a spectacular environment for work. There is a central core to house meeting rooms and other facilities as well as a 'leisure zone'.

The unusual space plan reflects the architect's desire for innovation. The bench desking, arranged in angled spines, provides a 2.5 metre (8 foot) length of desk per person that allows individuals to tailor their own work settings. This is an adaptable solution that can accommodate different space densities in an industry that never stands still – as Real Names discovered to its cost.

location San Francisco, USA **client** RealNames Corporation **completed** 2000 **total floor space (project 1)** 2,500 square metres (27,000 square feet) **(project 2)** 4,900 square metres (53,000 square feet) **staff (project 1)** 250 **(project 2)**300

1 Exposed services and dramatic use of lighting and colour are combined with materials that include fibreglass panelling to create impact and dynamism

1

2

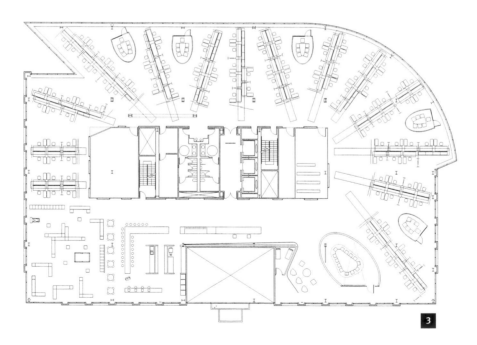

3

2 Spines of desks occupy
   the main workspaces;
   services such as power
   and data cabling are
   delivered from above
   through the centre of
   the furniture

3 Floor plan shows the
   desk spines arranged at
   varying angles to create
   an innovative landscape
   for the open-plan
   areas, interspersed
   with truncated, elliptical
   enclosed meeting pods

4 Server 'farms', usually
   relegated to basement
   computer rooms, are
   brought into the main
   reception area so that
   the technology that
   is the backbone of the
   business can be clearly
   seen through glazed
   partitioning

5 Detail of a meeting pod,
   whose translucent walls
   allow observers to see if
   the room is occupied and
   a meeting is in progress

4

5

124

6 Computer-generated
model of the second
building for RealNames,
where the theme of a
central core with spinal
workstations has been
reinforced with some
innovative new features

7 The double-height
structure, inserted into
the warehouse space,
provides a central core
of meeting spaces, café
areas and technology
rooms. Walls 10 metres
(33 feet) high are clad in
translucent fibreglass
with fluorescent
coloured lights behind

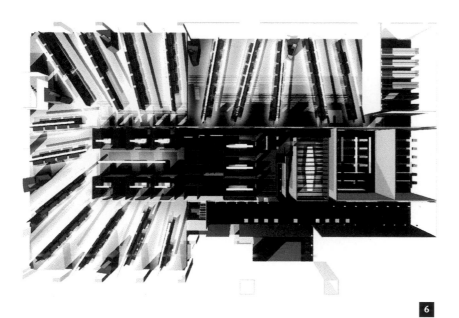

6

7

Philipp and Keuntje
Hamburg, Germany
feldmann + schultchen

126 A FORMER parish hall in central Hamburg is the unlikely location for a young, award-winning advertising agency, Philipp and Keuntje. Complete with a former milk bar as well as the old sexton's (church janitor's) house, the building offered a challenge to occupy. But the energy and drive of the agency were such that it put up with renovation works going on all around it to achieve the desired effect.

The result is a workplace in which the feeling of 'home' has been skilfully and intentionally maintained. Designers feldmann + schultchen left much of the 1960s interior intact, including striking glass bubble lamps. The hall's 5 metre (16 foot) high ceilings, wainscoted walls and full-height windows made it ideal to convert into a large, inspirational, central workspace for the agency's creative department.

To furnish the space, the design team made purpose-built units in wood and light green fabric, some reminiscent of restaurant or diner tables. The real innovation, however, is the 'constellation' of five work benches providing interconnected desk modules. Each unit has four 'mutually countered' desks formed from a series of interconnected U-shaped modules. This arrangement not only provides effective workstations but gives a dramatic symmetry to the interior of the hall.

Given the unique architectural challenge, the lighting needed to be purpose-designed for the project, and special light boxes giving daylight-quality illumination were made to follow the building's line. The ceiling resembles a strange circuit board, with raw concrete and interconnecting pipes linking the light boxes.

The sexton's house was converted into the accounts department, again with flexible, purpose-designed furniture. Scattered around the building, in the many small rooms, are mini-lounges or 'thinking corners' with casual or soft seating. A pantry and 'post office' in the reception area complete a scheme that reflects the trend to create work environments that have attributes of residential design. This 'house' really does provide a home for the agency – where people can share knowledge and ideas in an environment that feels more collegiate than corporate.

location Hamburg, Germany **client** Philipp and Keuntje **completed** 2001 **total floor space** 850 square metres (9,150 square feet) **staff** 50

1 Original 1960s light fittings have been combined with purpose-designed furniture to create the main working environment in this old parish hall. The desks are formed from a series of interconnected U-shaped modules

nodal: Philipp and Keuntje

2

4

3

2 The main reception
   desk, made out of
   concrete, dominates
   the entrance hall and
   connects to the wooden
   block that houses a coat
   cupboard and pantry

3 Juxtaposed alongside
   the work areas are
   social breakout spaces
   that provide more
   informal settings for
   collaboration

4 Purpose-designed light
   boxes follow the lines of
   the architecture. With
   metal pipes acting as
   connectors, the grid is
   like a circuit board

5 A 'thinking corner' with
   wall-mounted espresso
   machine: spaces like
   these are fitted into
   recesses all around
   the building

5

3 neighbourly

office as social landscape

Offices were once designed as workhouses, reflecting the idea that work was something to be endured rather than enjoyed. Some employees were not even allowed to converse, let alone to flirt or gossip. But, in the people-centred economy of the 21st century, imaginative new offices are emerging in which social interaction is encouraged rather than frowned on. The neighbourly office is designed as a social landscape to bring people together in a community of purpose. It is a complete corporate society and its repertoire of town squares, garden fences, entertainment zones, quiet spaces and lively bars increasingly mirrors the dynamic of the modern city, with its chance encounters, its colour and bustle. Here is a selection of office interiors that illustrates the neighbourly trend.

**Foote, Cone & Belding
Irvine, California, USA
Clive Wilkinson Architects**

132   WHEN advertising agency Foote, Cone & Belding Southern California decided to
sharpen its creative edge by moving to a more open and inspiring setting, its choice
of location and architect produced a landmark project offering a new 'waterfront'
angle on the office as a social quarter. The site was a former factory. The architect
was Clive Wilkinson, designer of an acclaimed Los Angeles scheme for a rival agency,
TBWA\Chiat\Day (see pages 192–97), occupying a similar giant warehouse space.

But whereas TBWA\Chiat\Day's office-as-city metaphor is
modelled on a slice of 1960s Greenwich Village, the Foote, Cone
& Belding office exploits the dramatic contrast in the old factory
between an orderly office section and an irregular, trapezoidal-
shaped manufacturing area to suggest a romantic relationship
between land and sea – even though no actual water is involved.

In the factory's former office area, double-height warehouse-
like space is occupied by dockside structures on the 'land side'.
In the manufacturing area, two 'floating' wooden structures
accommodate rooms needed to support adjacent work areas;
these are linked with a jetty-like bridge, which terminates 'at
sea', close to a rear staff entrance.

This is the office as seascape rather than cityscape, but
beyond the notional habourside Clive Wilkinson's design
scheme sails into more familiar waters, with rational provision
of offices without doors, focus rooms, project rooms and
support services, as well as a café, lounge space and editing
suite. Care has been taken to ensure that ideas travel round
the building quickly. From the front entrance a wide street
leads past a two-storey red display wall through an office
area to a 'dry dock', where public meeting
rooms are housed in steel-faced structures
and a raised boardroom is enclosed by
'walls' comprising 142 white surfboards.

This is a scheme that plays with
inspirational ideas but never forgets
its duty to provide a comfortable and
productive work environment. The result is
a voyage of discovery in which views from
the upper conference rooms onto the pale
trapezoidal shapes of green and blue
workdesks spreading below suggest an
agency determined to make waves.
location Irvine, California, USA **client**
Foote, Cone & Belding Southern California
completed August 2001 **total floor space**
9,310 square metres (101,200 square feet)
staff 300

1   View into café
    area emphasizes the
    neighbourly flavour
    of the project

2   Hanging sailboards,
    jetty-like structures
    and 'floating' features
    create an abstract
    metaphor of office
    as waterfront social
    quarter – without
    using any real water

1

3 Floor plan showing how an industrial factory has been transformed into a functioning creative agency. The trapezoidal former manufacturing area (right-hand side) is interpreted as a seascape and harbour front

4 View through double-height neighbourhood zone on 'land side' wing of building

5 A raised boardroom in the project's 'dry dock' offers a grotto-like enclosure within walls of suspended surfboards

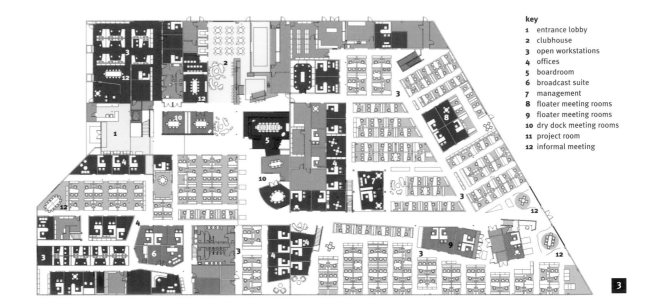

key
1 entrance lobby
2 clubhouse
3 open workstations
4 offices
5 boardroom
6 broadcast suite
7 management
8 floater meeting rooms
9 floater meeting rooms
10 dry dock meeting rooms
11 project room
12 informal meeting

6 View from upper
   conference level
   down onto 'seascape'
   of green and blue
   office desks

7, 8
   Views of the open
   upper-level meeting
   areas of Ping and
   Pong. Giant Y-shaped
   sculptural elements
   house TV monitors,
   audiovisual devices
   and speakers

9 Upper-level seating
   area with custom
   furniture

6

7

8

9

another.com
London, UK
Nowicka Stern

138   'SURF and turf' is the metaphor used to describe this small neighbourly office for an internet company, and the designers have translated the concept literally, laying grass in an area of the office. Using the cityscape as inspiration, they have created four team tables for work – 'surfing' the net – with spaces in between where there is no furniture nor spatial hierarchy, reflecting the shared nature of a park (the 'turf').

It is in this area, based loosely on New York's Central Park, that people are encouraged to meet, eat, rest, play and talk. The company has introduced the idea of the 'corporate picnic', an informal meeting to prompt creative thought and innovation. Continuing the park analogy, a set of swings has been crafted out of tractor seats, and these provide a very different welcome for visitors, designed to put them at ease on arrival.

The team tables cater well for an expanding flexible workforce that provides email address services for the digital age. In fact, another.com's emphasis on the virtual is part of the rationale for a design solution that focuses on the real. When a company operates in cyberspace, it is logical to bring its employees back to (a clod of) earth and create real spaces for work.

This approach reflects at a micro-level the concept of real neighbourhoods in typical urban environments with local shared amenities for recreation and communication. It suggests the model of the city as a basis for the future for the office; another.com has succeeded in bringing the outside in, to create a healthy balance of spaces for a demanding workforce.

location London, UK **client** another.com **completed** 2000
total floor space 250 square metres (2,700 square feet) **staff** 40

1 Floor plan showing the neighbourhoods and workspaces based around four team tables

2 Turf in the office: this is real grass that represents a park and builds on the theme of urban cityscapes as well as the metaphor of 'surf and turf' for this internet business

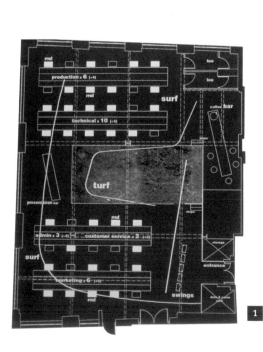

1

2

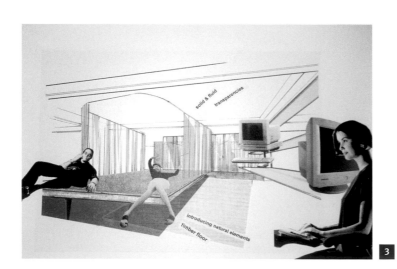

3 Concept and mood boards for the scheme design show the mix between recreation and communication that is synonymous with real urban neighbourhoods

4 Swings in the reception lift lobby provide visitor seating that is designed to put people at ease

Happy
Gothenburg, Sweden
White Arkitekter

142 THE brief from Happy, a Gothenburg-based design agency, was to create an office that would be 'intellectually liberating' and enhance the group dynamic through 'collective individualism'. In response, the architects White Arkitekter intentionally created a communal space that would accept paper on floors and drawings on walls – an environment that would not stifle Happy's creativity .

The work process is very much in the foreground, with the office's colour and vibrancy provided by the firm's ideas rather than by the interior architecture. Concealed beneath the surface of this paper-friendly setting are high-tech enablers, all part of a carefully framed stage set for work. Three quiet rooms and a glazed rooftop retreat offer places for contemplation and conference, while the rest of the space is split between collaborative zones and private cells.

The 'intensive care area' is designed to be a hive of activity: a shared space at the centre of the community. This idea of the creative cooperative is enriched by a small kitchen where, at the start of each day, staff share a communal breakfast. As well as shared environments, everyone is provided with an individual home or 'nest' – a small carrel that functions as a detached work unit for people and their possessions.

The workspace itself encourages people to use different kinds of workstations at different times of the day according to task. Common spaces and private cubicles offer alternative settings and show the contrast between public and private, collective and individual, performing and pondering.

Materials avoid the Swedish tradition of minimalism yet retain a neutral palette so that the focus comes from the people and their work. 'Non-colour' is the term used to describe the hues of white and clay that work with the Oregon pine to mould a calm and professional environment. The architects have created a flexible series of spaces for meetings, brainstorms and relaxation – and a subtly rich ambience that forms an unassuming but productive backdrop for Happy's work.
location Gothenburg, Sweden **client** Happy **completed** 2001 **total floor space** 8,100 square feet (750 square metres) **staff** 30

1 Roof of the former merchandise warehouse, where a rooftop box houses a meeting place with views over Kungsgatan

2 'Intensive care area' at the heart of the office – a paper-friendly hive of activity where people can spread out and work in a casual setting

1 2

3 Hues of white or
  'non-colour' provide
  a neutral backdrop

4 Circulation routes
  use Oregon pine to
  complement the white
  finishes and give the
  environment a calm
  and professional feel

4

5 Away from individual
'nests' people can use
a variety of shared
social settings

6 Axonometric shows
clusters of 'nests'
in the centre of the
space surrounded by
shared settings and
cellular offices

7 Enclosed spaces have
been imaginatively
designed with
purpose-made bench
seating upholstered
in quality fabric

146

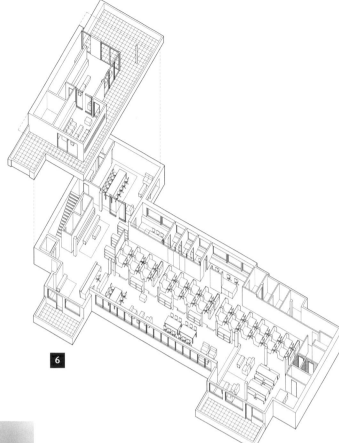

6

5

Exposure
London, UK
Creneau/Paul Daly

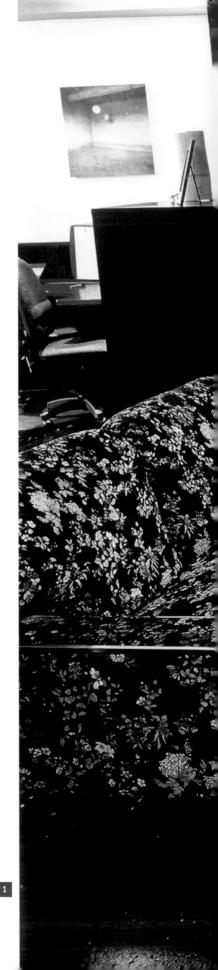

148 'LIVING at work' is a term used to describe the long-hours culture of young, image-conscious employees who don't leave work when day turns to night because their office is like a club and they're having such a good time. Fashion marketing agency Exposure reflects this trend. If you visit its West End office on a Friday evening, the DJs will be laying down the sound in the supercool black and red reception area – and the party will be in full swing.

When joint managing directors Raoul Shah and Tim Bourne moved the company to new West End offices in Little Portland Street in May 2000, they stripped the four-storey building back to its bare bones and worked with Belgian designer Will Erens of Creneau International to raid the flea markets and antique shops of Europe in search of the unorthodox and the original to furnish the new environment.

Standard workstations were off the agenda. Instead, each staff member was given an individual desk, albeit secondhand. The result is a richly eclectic interior designed to express the idea of 'a walk through the markets of the world'. Hybrid, invented styles such as 'Moroccan Techno' and 'Danish Punk' coexist without really blending. Indian fabrics jostle with an old Japanese tea steamer on wheels; chain mail curtains demarcate areas; two red crosses from First World War hospital tents adorn Shah's all-white private space.

This idea of a deliberate culture clash – with the accent on experiment and surprise – was subsequently carried through into a second phase, designed by Paul Daly and opened in June 2002. The third floor, fitted out for the agency's accounts and events teams, has an 'Andy Warhol meets Chinatown' feel, complete with graffiti-style stencils and hexagonal suspended ceiling units.

In a company where the receptionist greets visitors in a bizarre kitchen on wheels surrounded by cooking utensils, it can be said with some certainty that understated corporate modernity is not Exposure's thing. But the agency's racy, provocative mix of visual cultures has created a vibrant, club-like workplace like no other, which has contributed hugely to Exposure's rapid growth.
location London, UK **client** Exposure **completed** May 2000/June 2002 **total floor space** 1,100 square metres (11,500 square feet) **staff** 85

1 Exposure's third floor, designed by Paul Daly Studio, cultivates the idea of a deliberate culture clash in its eclectic choice of furnishings and decoration

Scenes from phase
one of the project,
designed by Creneau
International. The
theme is a stroll
through the markets

of the world. The
accent is an unusual
juxtaposition of
effects – ranging
from Cool Britannia
to Indian mysticism

Directors' offices. One
private room is adorned
with original wartime
Red Cross tent hangings;
another favours ornate
traditional furniture

and hexagonal ceiling
tiles adorn a dynamic
workspace

club environment for
the fashion marketing
agency's young staff

full of surprises

7

8

9

10

11

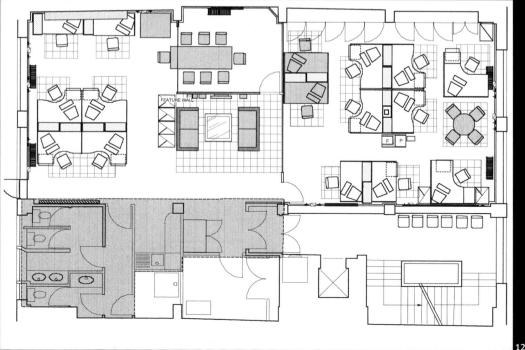

FEATURE WALL

F P

12

**Fritzsch & Mackat
Berlin, Germany
Mateja Mikulandra Mackat**

154 A FIRST-floor storage area in the former Schultheiss Brewery on Berlin's Prenzlauer Berg is the site of this intriguing office for a new, expanding advertising agency. The design has maintained the integrity of the brewery building but created a purposeful modern workplace. The architecture of the new office aims to reflect the culture and ethos of Fritzsch & Mackat with its young workforce and flat hierarchy.

The need for open and informal relations and fast channels of communication between employees directed the space plan. Account management and creatives are close to each other, but management is accessible, too, rather than physically separated. Only the production and finished art department is set apart, to emphasize a separation between creation and realization.

The outstanding feature is the conference room – placed at the heart of the agency – where brainstorms, presentations and decision-making take place. The drive for openness and transparency led to the construction of a translucent pod that hangs in the main work environment, making a dramatic and memorable place for collaboration.

This keg-formed conference room is built mainly of glass and 'floats' 4 metres (13 feet) above the employees at desks below. Elsewhere, furniture has been purpose-made from polycarbonate panels slotted into anodized aluminium frames, and only storage cabinets and some acoustic panels break up the open space. A minimalist café provides an environment for relaxation and an opportunity for 'boisterousness' – a contrast to the business-like atmosphere in work areas. In projecting itself as open, young, cooperative and progressive, the agency ruled out ostentatious gestures of success through expensive materials and hierarchical divisions of space. Instead, this office has been left as one large room, emphasizing the agency's philosophy and creating a communal conference room above. **location** Berlin, Germany **client** Fritzsch & Mackat **completed** 2001 **total floor space** 800 square metres (8,610 square feet) **staff** 25

1

2

1 The minimalist
reception area
features a curved
desk with backlit
panels that creates
a striking entrance
to the building

2 Main open-plan work
environment with a
dramatic translucent
pod that hangs in
space and serves as
the agency's main
conference room

neighbourly: Fritzsch & Mackat

3 Interior of the
conference pod that
provides a setting
for brainstorms and
presentations.
Its transparency
maintains the link
with the creative
work taking place
in the office below

4 Social space and café,
where staff can relax
in clean, uncluttered
surroundings that
contrast with the busy
work environment

4 Library area near the perimeter provides a quiet zone for concentrated work

5 Main circulation routes are generous and maintain the airy feel of this warehouse space

6 Bench workstations open out onto the communal central zone, where raised meeting pods provide places for privacy and interaction

4

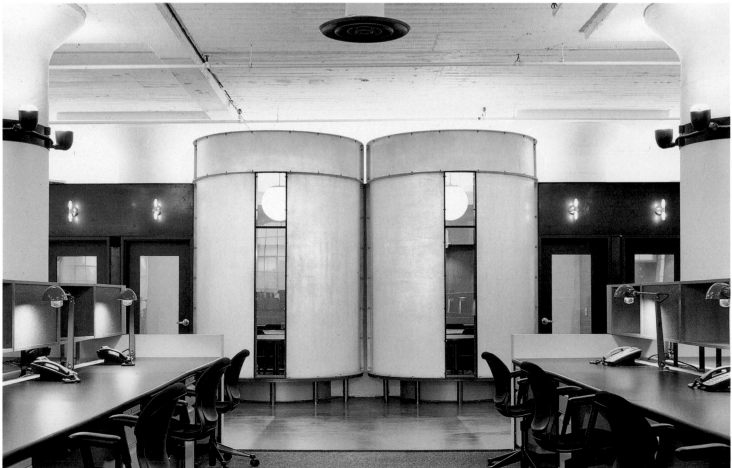

**Cellular Operations
Swindon, UK
Richard Hywel Evans
Architecture and Design**

162   CALL centres have been dubbed the 'sweatshops of the 21st century', so closely are they identified with high staff turnover, illness and absenteeism. This scheme for a call-centre company in Swindon totally reverses the trend with an imaginative environment designed to improve staff recruitment and retention.

The key to the project is the site in a semi-rural Wiltshire park just 3.2 kilometres (2 miles) from Swindon town centre. Here architect Richard Hywel Evans has created a building with a spectacular curved glass extension that has become a local high-tech landmark. The organic form of this three-storey glass sweep mirrors its natural surroundings. It appears to 'explode' from a crisply economical black box at the core of the building to snake around the site and rest against a base of polished boulders.

On the ground floor, operators can break out from their tight workstations to rest in naturally lit soft-seating areas against the curving glass façade that gives views of a lake. On upper floors is space for accounts, management, storage and subletting.

To deal with the unusual planar angles at the glass 'nose' of the call centre, client and architect collaborated to develop a slide-and-twist clamping solution based on a spider clamp made by automotive engineers. To avoid unwanted heat gain, they worked with a company that supplies jet engine blades to Boeing to develop a new system of blinds sitting on a solar tracking arm.

1 View of south elevation, showing how the building snakes along the side of the lake

Call centres are often hot and noisy. At Cellular Operations, cool air is piped from the nearby lake to desks through a series of vents, and sound is dampened by the use of freeform spatial layouts that avoid reverberating surfaces. Uniformed tea ladies with old-style trolleys have been reintroduced as social catalysts in the work environment. Even the toilets were designed as a technological experience, complete with electronic taps, heat-senstive urinals, mosaics and fibre optics.

2 Right up against the curved glass façade, breakout areas with soft seating are organized to exploit natural light and views. A curving wooden walkway divides people who are relaxing from those answering the telephone

The new £6.2 million call centre had the desired effect, dramatically cutting staff turnover by transforming a sweatshop into a social landscape.

location Swindon, UK **client** Cellular Operations **completed** January 2000 **total floor space** 3,700 square metres (40,000 square feet) **staff** 500

1

2

3 Architect and client
shared an interest
in automotive
engineering that
influenced the
ambitious form and
component-based
construction of
the two-level
office building

4 Second-floor plan

5 First-floor plan

6 Ground-floor plan

7 Section through two-
storey office area

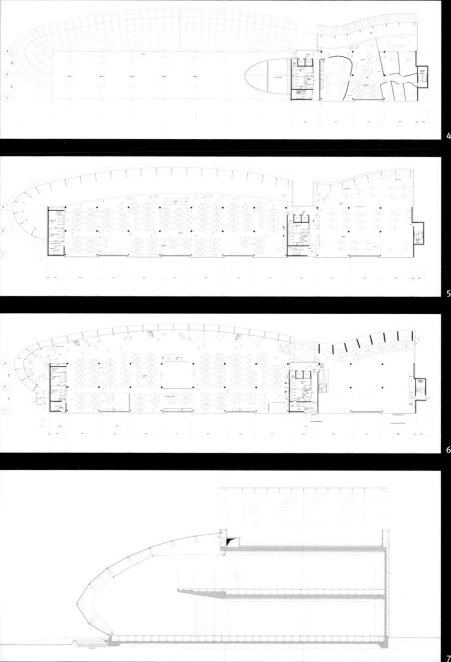

8 The building delights
   in making its technology
   explicit: networking
   equipment is exposed at
   the foot of a staircase

9, 10
   At Cellular Operations
   even the toilets are
   designed for amusement
   and relaxation

9

10

Beacon
Tokyo, Japan
Klein Dytham Architecture

168   WHEN three Japanese advertising agencies merged into one Tokyo-based firm, the
newly formed Beacon wanted to encourage as much social interaction between
employees as possible. A move downtown to the JR Tokyu Meguro Building, above
a new railway station, brought staff closer to the city's consumer centre and offered a
chance to create an environment where ideas could be shared and dialogue enhanced.

Klein Dytham's scheme for Beacon accentuates a sense of
openness and flexibility in a building with column-free floorplates
of 900 square metres (9,700 square feet) and dynamic views of the
train tracks to the north and south. Open-plan desking is laid out in
such a way that everyone can enjoy the natural light and stunning
panorama of the Tokyo skyline to the west. Meeting spaces and
multi-purpose areas are arranged against the core east-facing wall.

In this open environment – not even the directors have private
offices – different spaces are marked out by a ribbon device that
links one area to the next. Sometimes the ribbon acts as a ceiling
to a room; at other times it acts as a wall or screen. Each floor has
a different theme – Family, Woman, Man, Community, for example –
and the ribbon changes material according to which floor you are
on. On the Family floor, which revolves around a fully functioning
kitchen with cooking and laundry facilities, the ribbon is made
of wood. On the Woman floor, which has a hair and beauty salon
spilling out from an open stage, the ribbon is made of pink
snakeskin. On the male floor, the ribbon is made of steel.

The six directors and the company president work at a dining
table 12 metres (40 feet) long, and anyone in the agency can pull
up one of 20 dining chairs for a chat. The idea behind the project is
'*okarinasai*' or 'welcome home' – this is an agency that recognizes
the importance of good company
relations to business success.
location Tokyo, Japan **client**
Beacon **completed** 2002 **total**
floor space 4,300 square metres
(46,300 square feet) **staff** 350

1   The project uses a
    ribbon technique as
    a governing structural
    device to link one
    area to the next

2   In the reception area
    the ribbon creates a
    seating unit

3 Images along the top row reveal scenes from the themed 'Man' floor, which has a steel ribbon weaving through the space

4 Images along the middle row show different areas on the 'Woman' floor. The pink snakeskin-covered ribbon accommodates a beauty salon (left) and creates a loft-style bed (far right)

5 Images along the bottom row show the 'Family' area. Here a wooden ribbon creates furniture and structural elements

3

4

5

the 21st century office

6 Bringing people who had been in different agencies together in a single community of purpose was a key objective of the Beacon project. Here, the use of duck lights on a main 'dining table' – where the directors work and anyone in the agency can draw up a chair – adds a friendly touch

7 Social space offering excellent views of the Tokyo skyline

**Egg
Derby, UK
DEGW**

174 HIGH staff turnover is the curse of the call-centre industry. So when British financial services giant Prudential decided to build a new call centre in Derby for its Egg operation, the aim was to create a more engaging and less stressful environment than normal in order to attract and retain the young people needed to man the phones.

Built on a brownfield site, the scheme occupies one main floor, with a mezzanine level containing a staff restaurant and training areas. The building itself is nothing special: a standard high-tech industrial shed, albeit a cleverly shaped one. The real innovation is in the treatment of the interior spaces, which have been shaped according to a townscape design, complete with streets, squares, local neighbourhoods and even 'civic buildings'.

The civic buildings – giant breakout areas constructed as simple architectural forms – hold the key to this city-plan approach. They can accommodate 30 to 40 people at a time and provide a welcome retreat for staff during work breaks in seven-hour shifts.

Egg's call centre is divided into two wings and there are different breakout structures in each wing. Two-storey cubes are 'active' retreats offering diversions such as table football; single-storey spheres are 'passive' retreats – relaxing rooms with lower lighting levels and soft seating. Staff have been encouraged to decorate these spaces themselves.

The giant automated expanse of the call centre has been given other friendly touches such as brightly coloured hanging banners, which aid orientation, and a central piazza with trees that reach up into the mezzanine. An employee who hits a sales target can take time out on one of Egg's arcade-style electronic ski machines or spend time in the 'mental gym' – a computer learning room.

Within each 'neighbourhood', managers sit with teams, music plays and there is an accent on fun and competitiveness. There is a buzz and a team spirit about Egg, which has succeeded in reducing levels of staff turnover.

location Derby, UK **client** Prudential **completed** 1999 **total floor space** 9,200 square metres (100,000 square feet) **staff** 1,000

1 Within a standard industrial shell, coloured banners animate a call centre with a difference. The project is planned as a townscape complete with civic 'buildings' (see far left)

1

neighbourly: Egg

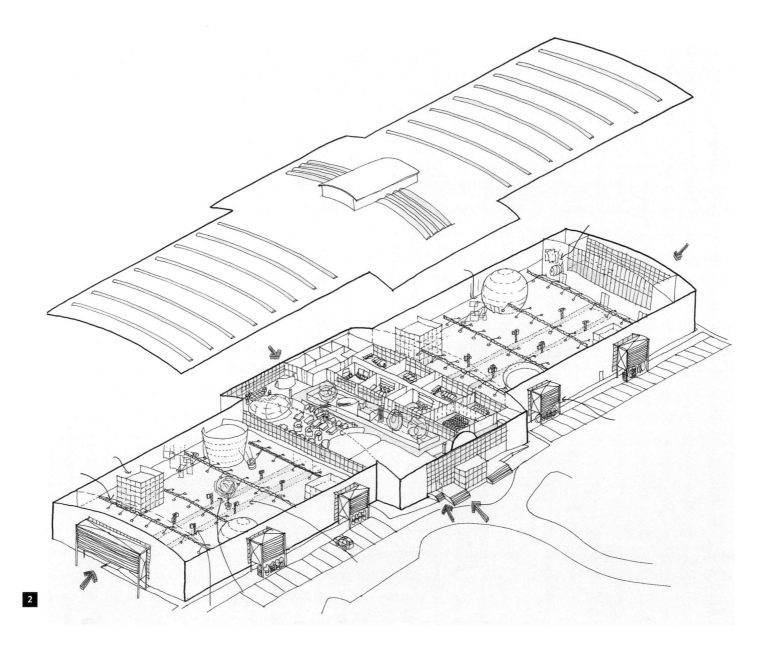

2

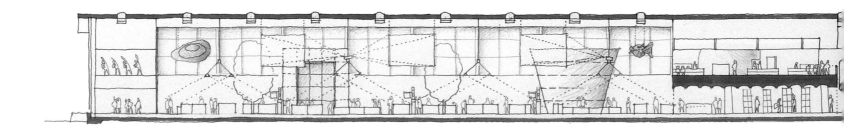

2 Scheme axonometric
shows how the
geometrically shaped
breakout pavilions
divide the space

3 Banners suspended
from an exposed
industrial-shed ceiling
aid orientation

4 Sketch view of Egg
interior suggests
social interaction
at work

5 Longitudinal section
reveals the extent
of the scheme

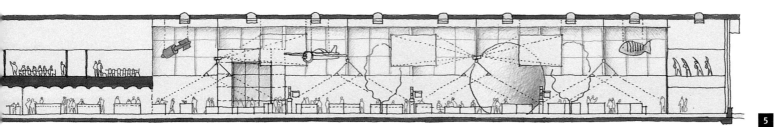

7

6 Giant chillout zone
where call-centre
operators can take a
break between shifts.
Staff are encouraged
to decorate the walls

7 Social zone with
circular seating
unit fosters a
neighbourly ethos
despite the large
scale of the operation

AV62 Arquitectos
Barcelona, Spain
AV62 Arquitectos

180   THIS scheme remodels and refurbishes a former textile warehouse in Barcelona to create an office for an architectural practice, AV62 Arquitectos. Within a single commercial property, the space has been designed to be shared by two different teams working independently of each other. What could have been a difficult project resulting in disputes between neighbours operating in close proximity is skilfully resolved to create a small, harmonious work community.

The entire space, which is virtually a rectangle, has been divided in two, and an area providing access (through the courtyard of the building) and services (toilets and kitchen) has been sited in the central strip. In the reception lobby is a bench for visitors and a panel on the wall that graphically describes the activities of the practice.

The key to the project is a single piece of furniture that articulates the space – a long, narrow stainless-steel table on two levels, which provides the basic work spaces and demarcates areas for different functions. These areas, which include a small administrative office, a model-making section and a meeting room, are divided visually by glass and translucent panels and by an orange-coloured sliding screen. At the point where the level of the table changes there is a zone containing computer workstations.

Storage and library facilities are provided by furniture situated flush with the walls. To keep things in order, each person in the office has a storage chest on wheels under their desk for personal materials and belongings. All the flooring is of natural eucalyptus wood treated with a water-soluble varnish, and all the walls and ceilings are painted off-white.

This is a scheme that does the simple things well, using furniture to divide space and manage work functions in a calm and professional manner. It provides a setting for neighbours to coexist in a compact space while subtly promoting the qualities of good architectural practice.

location Barcelona, Spain **client** AV Arquitectos **completed** 2001 **total floor space** 190 square metres (2,000 square feet)

1 Floor plan reveals division of space

2 View of entrance lobby showing use of translucent panels, full-height joinery and simple wood finishes

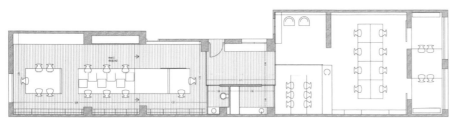

1

2

neighbourly: AV62 Arquitectos

tek/chər), n. 1. the profession
open areas, communities, and
tions and environments, usually
esthetic effect. The professional
often include design or selection
corations, supervision of construc-
mination, restoration, or remodel-
gs. 2. the character or style of
re of Paris; *Romanesque archi-*
r process of building; construction.
uct of architectural work, as a
collectively. 6. the structure of
re of a novel. [< L architectūr(a).

3

4

5

3 A graphic display in the lobby defines the nature of the architectural practice

4 Interior details show quality craftsmanship in this skilfully designed shared office

5 View of main workspace. A long table articulates the space with backlit panels to divide different functions

neighbourly: AV62 Arquitectos

Claydon Heeley Jones Mason
London, UK
Ushida Findlay Architects

184 THE traditional image of an advertising agency office is rich with glass, chrome, leather and marble to impress visiting clients. But when marketing communications firm Claydon Heeley Jones Mason decided to revamp five floors of its Battersea office, the brief to architects Ushida Findlay emphasized the organization's organic internal culture, especially the need to encourage fluidity and interaction, rather than an external craving for attention.

The result is an imaginative and sometimes humorous scheme that uses inexpensive materials (including mild steel, PVC, rubber and laminated medium-density fibreboard), bespoke desking solutions and unusual planning geometries to create a workplace that aims to make staff feel valued and inspired.

The new mood starts in the first-floor reception area, where rolled steel ribbons move through the space – a silver ribbon reflecting the River Thames, which can be seen through the window, and an orange one highlighting the agency's corporate colour. These flowing steel strands become a mechanism to demarcate different spaces – reception, café and client waiting area – without resorting to the usual modern design clichés.

However, despite the showstopping flourish of the reception, the key to the project is behind the scenes in the work areas, and in the requirement for flexible team-based working. The architects designed a series of six-person desk clusters arranged according to an unorthodox geometry (30°/60°, as opposed to the usual 45°/90°), grouped in the centre of the floorplate away from windows to reduce glare on computer monitors. This geometry defines all other aspects of the scheme: the position of ancillary space and edge storage as well as that of the bespoke edge seating and meeting tables in horseshoe-shaped alcoves.

With its bright colours and organic shapes – work areas have interlocking orange and green desks on a blue rubber flooring – this is a project that is unafraid to experiment with the expected view of what an advertising agency should look like. Ultimately, its defining steel ribbons become a metaphor for the agency's creative process rather than simply its outward image.

location London, UK **client** Claydon Heeley Jones Mason
completed 2001 **total floor space** 1,700 square metres
(18,500 square feet) **staff** 220

1 View into the Battersea building of a London agency located close to the River Thames, with the silver reception 'ribbon' clearly visible

2 The ribbon device provides seating and displays the agency showreel in the first-floor reception space

1

2

3 Breakout area in a
scheme designed to
encourage interaction

4 Open-plan six-person
workstations are
clustered to support
teamworking

5 The ribbon connects
the café with the
client waiting areas

6 Upper-floor
conference room

7 Upper-floor plan
showing the open
work area sandwiched
between conference
space and plant room

8 First-floor plan.
Behind the reception
area, six-person
workstations show
the unorthodox
geometry of the
desk clusters

6

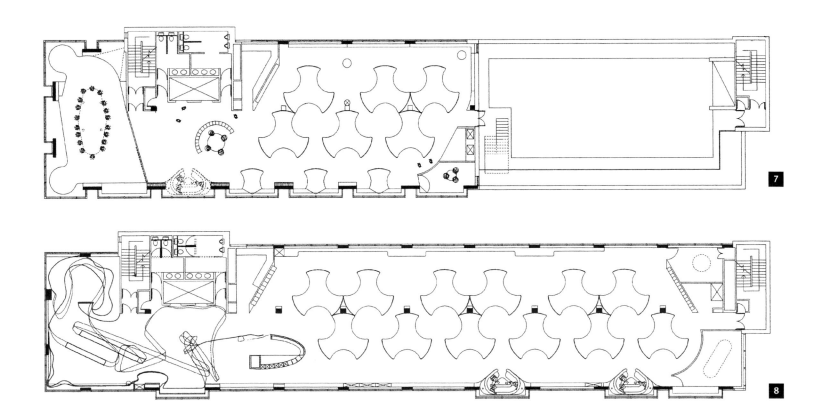

7

8

neighbourly: Claydon Heeley Jones Mason

**DVD Innovation Centre
Dortmund, Germany
Planungsgruppe Drahtler**

188   IT IS not often that an architect gets to occupy its own office scheme. But in creating Dortmund's new DVD Innovation Centre, Planungsgruppe Drahtler has also designed a workspace for itself. The building was commissioned by EMF New Media, and comprises offices, production suites and a private museum that is open to the public. The whole building is occupied by EMF, apart from the ground floor, where the architect has designed a work environment that suits its team-based ethos.

Clusters of three people share a workstation configuration in an area kept open to encourage collaboration between teams working on different projects. Furniture provides the only division of space, apart from an innovative 'red box' that has been built in the centre of the office. This feature creates a visual focus and has been designed as a 'veil' to conceal the multitude of grey, plastic-encased technology boxes, from plotters to photocopiers, that normally 'pollute' the office environment. In clustering equipment, the architect has also made a natural social focus where serendipitous meetings can take place.

Finishes include oakwood flooring and a concrete ceiling left exposed to show the quality of construction. Panelling on the interior walls uses external metal panels to bring the outside in. Adding drama is an impressive glass cube sculpture by Thomas Emde that dominates the museum adjacent to the office space.

The project is a good example of the division of space into neighbourhoods that suit small teams (in this case, teams of three). It also illustrates how effectively an office service area, normally relegated to a spare corner cupboard, can be placed centrally on the floorplate and given prominence with dramatic red translucent walls to create a focal point.

location Dortmund, Germany **client** EMF New Media Company **completed** November 2000 **total floor space** 2,250 square metres (24,220 square feet) **staff** 17

1 Exterior of the Innovation Centre shows the office areas and Planungsgruppe Drahtler's workplace on the ground floor

2 The 'red box' conceals office equipment and technology behind a translucent wall

neighbourly: DVD Innovation Centre

3

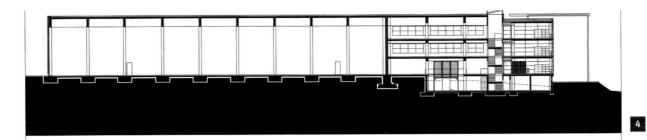

4

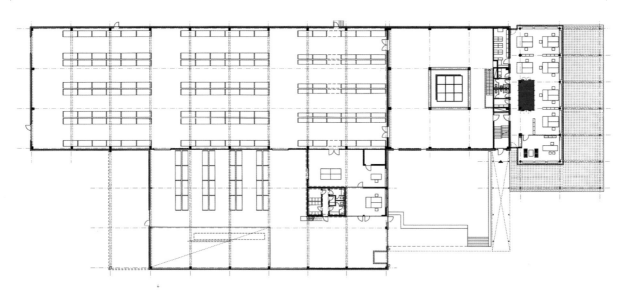

5

3 The museum adjacent to
the office block houses
an impressive glass cube
sculpture by Thomas Emde

4 Section and floor plan
of the building, showing
the office areas on
the far right-hand side

5 The semi-open-plan
workstations were
each designed
for teams of three

TBWA\Chiat\Day
Los Angeles, USA
Clive Wilkinson Architects

192   WHEN the staff of agency TBWA\Chiat\Day moved into architect Clive Wilkinson's new advertising 'city' in a remodelled warehouse in the Playa Vista area of Los Angeles, it felt like they were coming home after sleeping rough for a long time. At the company's former premises in Venice, California – designed by Frank Gehry with a binocular portal by Claes Oldenburg – an unpopular 'hoteling' system had made for a dissatisfied workforce unable to call any part of the office its own.

Wilkinson and the agency's management were determined not to make the same mistake again. The new scheme set out to create an entire urban neighbourhood modelled on Greenwich Village, in which everyone would have their own personal place to work as well as access to shared 'public' amenities such as a park, basketball court and café spaces.

The city metaphor is convincing. Entry to the agency is via a metal-clad gatehouse, which accommodates a reception area and a gallery for the agency's work. Two pedestrian 'tubes' each 15.25 metres (50 feet) in length suggest arrival in a city from the inside of an aircraft.

Visitors emerge from these the narrow entry capsules to confront an urban vista complete with multiple levels, landmark structures, an 'irregular' skyline, tree-lined spaces and a main street that bisects the ground floor. On either side of the street, the agency's creative department is housed in prefabricated 'cliff dwellings' – bright yellow constructions of steel, concrete and metal decking. At an upper level, bridges and ramps link a series of mezzanines.

Team space is not ignored in a project dedicated to restoring a sense of community to a fractured and fractious workforce. Special custom-designed workstations called Nests encircle the city centre, housing project teams. Project dens are created in ethereal double-height fabric enclosures suspended from above.

Although the project was completed at the end of 1998, it was widely heralded as 21st century in its thinking. Wilkinson's scheme did more than perhaps any other to bring down the curtain on a series of ruthless, space-saving, desk-sharing schemes in the 1990s, reviving a more generous, neighbourly approach that has been widely studied and emulated since.
location Los Angeles, USA **client** TBWA\Chiat\Day
completed 1998 **total floor space** 11,000 square metres
(120,000 square feet) **staff** 550

1

1 View of the project's
'central park',
complete with
planting, street
furniture – and
even a red British
telephone box.
Yellow prefabricated
'cliff dwellings'
can be seen in
the background

2 Ground-floor plan

key
1 gatehouse reception
2 ramp
3 main street
4 cliff dwellings
5 central park
6 surf bar
7 basketball court
8 project den tent structure

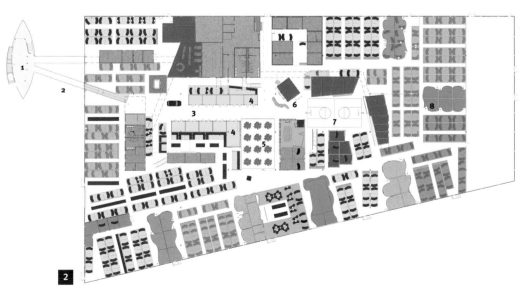

neighbourly: TBWA\Chiat\Day

3 Project dens occupy full-height tensile structures hung from above. Clustered workstations, known as Nests, were developed specially for the project by the architect in collaboration with Steelcase

4 Stacked metal 'cliff dwellings' to accommodate agency staff were prefabricated off-site

5 View of the art studio
at the rear of the 'cliff
dwellings'. A café
and conference rooms
can be reached on
the mezzanine level

6 A basketball court
forms part of a
convincing Greenwich
Village metaphor
for the entire project

7 Close-up view of the
Nest workstations,
which address both
individual and team
requirements

8 View from the
gatehouse reception
desk down the twin
pedestrian tubes
through which
everyone must travel
to reach the main
work community. The
concept is based on
simulating arrival
in the office 'city' from
the narrow capsule
of an aircraft

6

7

8

4 nomadic

office as distributed workspace

Offices were once contained by time, place and space. People commuted to and from city-centre high-rises at set hours. But, in the technology-driven economy of the 21st century, offices are no longer dependent on location. Much work now takes place outside the traditional corporate building – and at every hour of the day and night. Portable communications devices and the internet have allowed work patterns to become more fluid. New environments are needed to make the workers of this new economy more productive. The nomadic office is geographically distributed across the spectrum of people's lives – from home and high street to airport lounge and serviced club. It offers real choices in terms of the balance between work and the rest of life. The following selection of interiors expresses the nomadic working concept through a series of settings and destinations.

IoD at 123
London, UK
hemingwaydesign

200 AS A place for company directors to meet and work in London's Pall Mall, the Institute of Directors (IoD) is part of the establishment, and its style is exactly what you would expect of a venerable institution: leather armchairs, grand marble staircase and impressive oil paintings. But Gerardine and Wayne Hemingway's design for the new IoD space at 123 Pall Mall, just along the road, breaks this mould. It brings with it a contemporary design approach to nomadic work, meeting the need of senior executives for temporary workspace with shared amenities and good technology support.

The environment provides a range of settings that cater for the different requirements of nomadic workers – from solo spaces to meeting areas. It aims to raise the productivity of people who have to work away from their offices, by providing everything that is available in an office but in a communal, 'drop-in' environment.

One area uses a rail-travel metaphor by recreating a typical train carriage seat with overhead luggage rack, while other settings are more reminiscent of a corporate meeting room environment. Pinstriped upholstery injects a sense of humour into the space, perhaps reflecting the designer's background in fashion.

Alongside these collaborative spaces are a series of small booths that allow people to use their laptops, recharge equipment and connect to the internet. Innovations include mobile phone recharging booths and wireless headsets for listening to television news without disturbing others.

As in any good nomadic space, service and familiarity are crucial. Top caterer Leith's provides food and drink, from cocktails to sushi. As the 'club' is for members only, people become familiar with the space and the others who use it. IoD at 123 is backed by other benefits for members, from training and a library to networking events and talks, so this nomadic space is part of a greater whole – an executive guild that looks after everything from members' career development and insurance to the provision of places to work while away from the office.
location London, UK **client** Institute of Directors
completed 2001 **total floor space** 160 square metres
(1,760 square feet) **staff** 250

1 Panoramic view showing the main reception area and café, as well as the corridor of private work booths leading down into the body of the space. This area is the meet-and-greet point for visitors and a place for support and office services

2 The basement area provides further areas for work as well as bookable rooms for meetings or presentations. Innovations include remote-control massage chairs to relax and soothe stressed company executives

2

3 Seating and furniture
offer people a choice
of work settings and
dictate the style and
formality of meetings

4 The main area on the
ground floor has
individual booths
for private work as
well as tables for
meetings. A plasma
screen broadcasts
news channels that
can be listened to on
wireless headphones,
while a wireless
data network allows
people to connect
to the internet from
laptops in any
location. There are
even free recharging
'lockers' for mobile
phones

Mercaders Building
Barcelona, Spain
Enric Miralles and Benedetta
Tagliabue

206   HOME offices are often the poor relations of their corporate cousins. Improvised
and tucked away in attics or spare bedrooms, they can be uninspiring and too rarely
provide truly productive and stimulating places for work. The Mercaders Building
in Barcelona, however, breaks this mould and creates a real place for work at home.

Architects Miralles and Tagliabue wanted to maintain the
atmosphere and feel of a dilapidated country house, while at
the same time renovating the space to provide an effective
environment in which they themselves could live and work.

The building had been used as a warehouse, and much of
the original interior had been destroyed. The designers set out
to create a feeling of mobility and coherence without formality.
The home office is at the heart of the apartment. It is located
at the centre of a floor that forms a continuous loop around a
courtyard. This external space gives the building an equilibrium
and central focus as well as direct access from the street.

Original wall coverings have been retained, and these
contrast dramatically with the elegant shared desk and
accessories. Modern floor finishes have been creatively layered
with original ones to orientate and organize the environment
and emphasize the sense of continuous space. Old tiles have
been relaid on top of rebuilt floors and arranged to resemble
rugs between areas of oak block flooring. This strange geometry
helps to articulate the space.

New partitions have been made to work like curtains and,
with the furniture, to demarcate individual spaces. The spatial
description has been interpreted literally in a large oak table –
with a fixed central section and a complex array of folding flaps
– which dominates the entrance hall and 'represents' the house.
Even the group of classic Danish Poul Henningsen-designed light
fittings for the library builds on the theme of decaying grandeur.

The project demonstrates how an innovative design solution
can work well within an historic building form, delivering
an unusual and rewarding interior that provides a productive
place for work.

location Barcelona, Spain **client** Miralles and Tagliabue
total floor space 375 square metres (4,035 square feet)

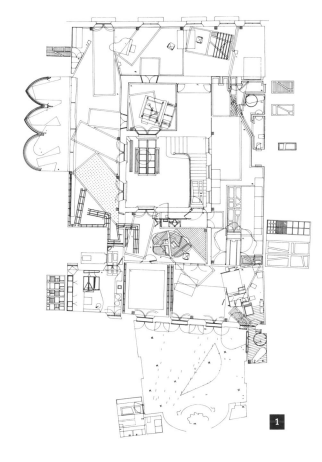

1 Floor plan of the first-
   floor flat, showing
   the juxtaposition
   of an innovative
   and original design
   solution with an
   historic building form.
   Modern floor finishes
   are creatively layered
   with original ones
   to orientate and
   organize the space

2 The home office at
   the heart of the flat,
   where original wall
   coverings contrast
   with the elegant
   shared desk and
   accessories. The
   workspace is located
   at the centre of a
   floor that forms
   a continuous loop
   around a courtyard

208

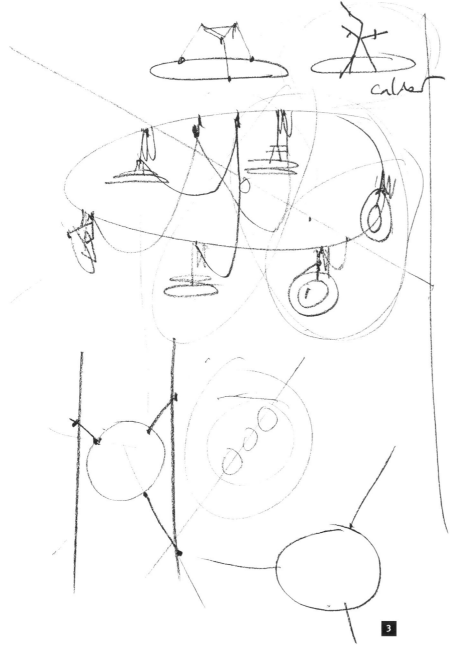

3

3 Concept sketch for
the light fitting that
dominates the room
and builds on the theme
of decaying grandeur.
The building's formal
lines are softened by
the complex form of
this piece of innovative
industrial design

4 The architects wanted to
maintain the atmosphere
and feel of a dilapidated
country house in the heart
of the city, while at the
same time renovating
the space to provide an
effective environment in
which to live and work.
The tensions between old
and new, rural and urban,
home and work, give the
scheme its distinction

4

nomadic: Mercaders Building

Westferry Studios
London, UK
CZWG Architects

210 THIS enterprising scheme pioneers mixed-use development for living and working in Britain. It addresses the social regeneration of depressed urban areas through the provision of low-cost units for start-up businesses. Westferry is based on the Isle of Dogs in London Docklands, just a stone's throw from the giant Canary Wharf office development. But, rather than luring multinationals and major financial institutions, it has been designed to attract fledgling craft, design and media firms to a communal environment offering cheap living accommodation within flexible shell work units.

The scheme is the brainchild of architect Dickon Robinson, development director of the Peabody Trust, a housing association and regeneration agency. Robinson commissioned designers CZWG to make Westferry, located next door to a Docklands Light Rail station, stand out as a landmark in the rundown area.

CZWG grouped a total of 27 live-work units on four floors around a courtyard, using a robust industrial language of brick, concrete and metal. Unit sizes range from 46 to 77 square metres (490 to 830 square feet). If the aesthetic tone evokes the workhouse, there is no denying the generous deal on offer to business tenants. The rent is subsidized for the first three years to enable new businesses to get off the ground. As Peabody Trust explains, the Westferry incubator is 'available for Londoners on low incomes but with big ideas'. All tenants are obliged to leave after five years to enable the development continually to 'seed' new enterprises.

As a building, Westferry reflects a basic approach to the complex issues of living and working – how units are subdivided to accommodate the two functions has required the attention of subsequent design studies. But there is no denying the raw energy of this hybrid concept nor its tough-minded execution.
location London, UK **client** Peabody Trust **completed** 1999 **total floor space** 3,508 square metres (37,760 square feet)

1 Westferry encases its live-work units behind a giant brick façade that spells out the name of the project in bold capital letters 9 metres (30 feet) high. The name can be clearly seen by travellers on the adjacent Docklands Light Rail line

2 Inside the Westferry development 27 live-work units are based around a courtyard. A robust industrial aesthetic dominates. A central scaffold tower is positioned to hold an as yet unrealized digital billboard

1

2

nomadic: Westferry Studios

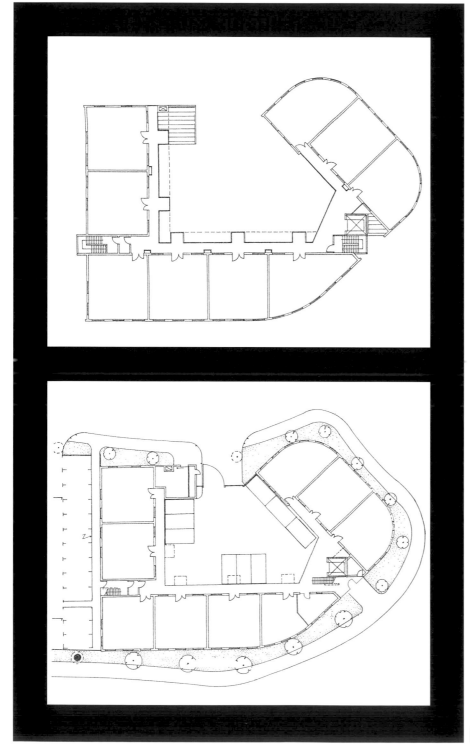

3

3 First- and third-floor
plans show the
rational geometry
of units

4 A standard live-work
unit that has been
adapted for use by
a fledgling fashion
entrepreneur

5 Live-work unit prior
to fitout – a blank
canvas for new
tenants to fill in

Virgin Atlantic
New York, USA
W1 Studio and TsAO & McKown

214   WITH the opening of the new Terminal 1 at New York's John F. Kennedy Airport, Virgin Atlantic wanted to make a statement in its executive lounge. Having worked with the international airline for a number of years, Patrick Hegarty at W1 Studio used his experience of the Virgin brand to collaborate with New York-based TsAO & McKown to create this vibrant and distinctive project.

Dramatic 5 metre (16 foot) high ceilings across the entire space of 550 square metres (6,000 square feet) present a scale and feel reminiscent of New York's skyscrapers, and the designers intentionally maintained the volume of space by using partitions only at the perimeter where necessary. The dramatic setting of the lounge provides full-height glazing that overlooks the runway and offers views across the Hudson river to downtown Manhattan and Wall Street.

Fabrics and finishes echo the geography of the Big Apple – with pinstriped upholstery used to reflect the financial district, denim used for the Greenwich Village feel of midtown, and silk to represent the Madison Avenue feel of uptown. The melting pot that is Manhattan is reflected in the interior, with furniture from around the globe, including eclectic seating from Sweden, Italy, France and Belgium, juxtaposed with design classics.

The use of a former American banker's desk (bought at auction) as the reception desk completes the innovative choice of furniture. And new thinking extends to the function of the reception area itself where – rather than having frustrated or angry passengers hovering round the desk – Virgin staff give customers a cordless phone and call them in the lounge when their query or need has been dealt with.

Many airport lounges adopt enclosed spaces as the solution for working on the move. Here, Virgin prefers to allow a distributed approach where work can happen in any setting. Nevertheless, a central business area in the middle of the floor provides some semi-enclosed spaces with acoustic privacy away from the bar and restaurant areas. The sheer scale of the lounge provides for more seats than can ever be needed, and from any of these places people have access to power and data for laptop use. This is a scheme that sets new standards in providing an eclectic mix of appropriate, innovative and attractive work settings for nomadic workers in a busy transport hub.

location New York, USA **client** Virgin Atlantic Airways **completed** April 2000 **total floor space** 550 square metres (6,000 square feet)

1   The classic 1960s Globe chair designed by Aarnio provides a stimulating setting for phone calls or contemplative thought

2   A row of Globes has been placed along the perimeter, giving people vistas across airside spaces, reinforcing the location and providing the executive with a theatre of activity or seclusion from the rest of the business lounge

1

3 View of the lounge from the mezzanine shows the scale of the space and the range of settings for formal and informal work. The eclectic mixture of furniture is intentional, with modern Knoll pieces such as the Eames Aluminium Group chair juxtaposed with more classical pieces such as the Pfinter lounge chair

4 Small booths for telephone use are part of the elliptical business desk that forms a central destination and hub for work

5 These innovative work units are formed from curved wooden panels that reflect the heritage and feel of New York libraries. Booths provide a semi-private space for laptop work

nomadic: Virgin Atlantic

Ocubis
London, UK
Magyar Marsoni Architects

218 MOST serviced offices rented for short periods by nomadic workers to suit changing work patterns are anonymous and mundane. Ocubis, located in the former Polish Club in Knightsbridge, decided to distinguish itself from other, similar offices through a bold investment in design. The concept took inspiration from designer Philippe Starck's work for Ian Schrager's hotels, where grand and often imposing public areas lead to more functional rooms behind. Ocubis set out to create a dramatic arrival with a double-height reception area complete with sweeping glass staircase.

The Grade II listed building presented a challenge to architects Magyar Marsoni, who chose to use the tension between the classical building and a modernist interior to their advantage. The project juxtaposes old and new to good effect. Nothing is hidden, and the visitor is taken on a journey through the space that is described as a series of 'episodes'. Even dull interior corridors have been given presence by the insertion of glass boxes and special lighting.

The building has 58 rentable rooms. At its heart is a communal area for meeting and greeting that has shared facilities such as conference rooms; the intention is to provide a relaxed place to meet, eat and drink, with a shared dining table supported by a kitchen. This 'point of arrival' is a focus for secretarial and reception services, and an internet café sits inside a mezzanine glass box in the space. (The original scheme included amenities in the basement such as a gym, but these were not built.)

Branding was key to the solution, and graphic designers Gregory Bonner Hale worked alongside the architects to ensure that Ocubis (also known as 64 Knightsbridge) is handsomely distinctive. The result is a facility that is a world away from the second-hand space in cheap locations that many serviced offices inhabit. Ocubis sets itself apart through its location and commitment to design and quality. It provides a statement building with its sense of arrival, grandeur and opulence for nomadic workers in start-up or breakaway businesses that would not normally be associated with such premises.

location London, UK **client** Ocubis Serviced Offices **completed** 2001 **total floor space** 1,400 square metres (15,000 square feet)

1 Concept sketch of the main entrance hall showing the double-height space and connections between the different settings such as meeting rooms and breakout spaces

2 The reception area, complete with a dramatic new staircase, projects a grandeur that would be unaffordable to most occupants of serviced offices. It creates an imposing public space and point of arrival

nomadic: Ocubis

3

3 By integrating old and new, the architect created a tension that has been used to inject drama into the environment. Shared facilities such as a dining table and kitchen provide communal space that brings people together from their different businesses

4 The concept was to combine impressive public areas and shared social spaces with more functional work environments. The design created a series of 'episodes' that draw people through the building

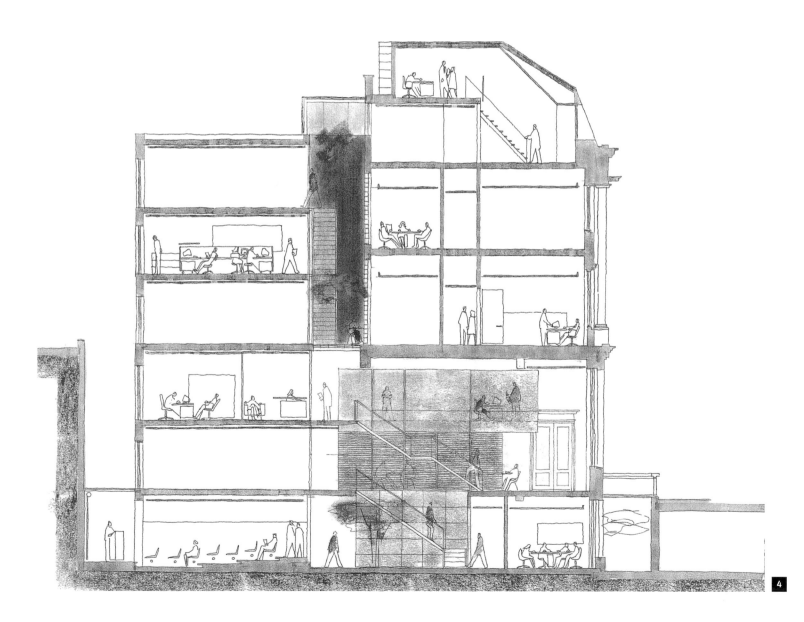

4

Teleworking Village and
Internet Home, Italy
Giancarlo De Carlo/
The Studio & Partners

222　THE technological revolution is fast liberating work from the traditional workplace, and one of its effects in continental Europe has been a growth in the popularity of teleworking. Two projects unveiled in Italy in 2001 caught the mood of interest in high-tech working from home, integrating new internet services in the fabric of old buildings.

In the first project, architect Giancarlo De Carlo – best known for his delicate historic work in restoring the Renaissance city of Urbino, masterminded the conversion of a 12th-century Italian hilltop village into a unique teleworking community.

The compact village of Colletta di Castelbianco in Liguria, northern Italy, was abandoned in the 1930s and left to ruin. In 1992 its derelict homes were acquired and an ambitious development plan undertaken to create 70 self-contained apartments in the shell of the old settlement.

De Carlo describes his approach as a 'crustacean system' – retaining the shell but altering the interior completely. Thus, outwardly, Colletta looks every inch the medieval hilltop jewel commanding magnificent views of the Italian countryside. Internally, every simple, modern apartment is equipped with broadband cables providing permanent internet access. It is perfect for the modern knowledge worker who wants access to the global media village from an inspirational rural retreat.

In the second project, five leading companies in design and services (Ariston Digital Wrap, BTicino, Cisco Systems, Luceplan and Molteni) teamed up to create the Internet Home – an experimental environment in which all the functions of the house are controlled via the web.

Based in a city-centre building in Milan's Piazza Diaz, just a few metres from the famous Duomo, the project was launched at the 2001 Milan Furniture Fair. Like the Colletta apartments, it is a scheme that demonstrates a fusion of refined Italian taste and traditional materials with the enabling technologies of the information age.
locations Colletta and Milan, Italy **completed** 2001

1　Inside the internet café serving the Colletta community

2　The 12th-century village of Colletta di Castelbianco Is the historic setting for a modern teleworking community

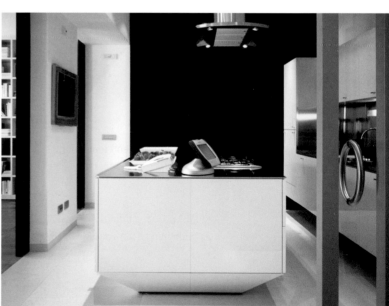

3 Inside the Internet
Home presented at
the Milan Furniture
Fair in 2001: views of
bedroom and study

4 Kitchen and living
areas are also web-
enabled, making
this environment a
seamless integration
of living and working

Cathay Pacific
Hong Kong, China
John Pawson

224 The business lounge for Cathay Pacific is located in the South concourse of one of the wings of Sir Norman Foster's magnificent Chek Lap Kok Airport in Hong Kong. The dramatic space has been skilfully slotted into the building envelope and provides a series of different settings for work.

As Hong Kong is Cathay's main international hub, no expense was spared to give its customers a premier environment for both work and leisure. The intent was to provide a real place to do work rather than simply a glorified waiting area for people about to board their planes. As well as the usual bars and restaurant facilities, and the shower cabanas with their private water features, the architect has created personal space for business travellers and designed a hybrid workplace for study and contemplation.

Technology has been carefully integrated into the environment so that the space does not resemble a typical office with its mass of equipment, but reflects the calm serenity demanded by most travellers. Materials are intentionally subdued, with black African granite used for both the floor and claddings, contrasting with slatted timber panels and illuminated Japanese paper screens that are lit by fibre optics.

The environment provides a series of tables for work and assumes that business people will have their laptops with them. This is an unusually effective example of a transport hub as nomadic work destination. It combines all the functionality of a conventional office with a welcome sanctuary from the hustle and stress of airport life.

location Chek Lap Kok Airport, Hong Kong, China **client** Cathay Pacific Airways **completed** 1999

1

1, 2
Executive lounges in airports now provide people with effective places to work. Foster's stunning Chek Lap Kok terminal is the setting for Pawson's interior workspace; a place for concentrated work, in an environment that preserves the feeling of being in an airport

nomadic: Cathay Pacific

**Granada Workspace
UK
BDG McColl**

226 SO-CALLED 'road warriors' spend a large proportion of their working lives in their cars. These nomadic workers have historically had to work 'on the fly', in their cars or at tables in roadside fast-food restaurants. But now Granada, the company that runs many motorway service areas in the UK, has joined forces with technology giant BT to create Workspace, a destination for business people on the road.

Workspace has been developed to provide a productive place for work while on the move as well as a connection point to corporate networks for email and data. BDG McColl set out to design an environment that would give the travelling executive a real place to work that was similar to a 'traditional' office. From the familiar service station concourse, business people can step into an oasis of calm and tranquillity, away from the noise and hubbub of motorway life.

The Workspace concept is divided into two zones and includes spaces for 'hot desking' or meetings as well as a 'communications hub' for corporate connectivity. A main reception offers meet-and-greet facilities as well as access to photocopiers, fax machines and printers. A plasma screen broadcasts business news, while a café delivers food and drink. For a longer stay, the second zone provides a pay-as-you-go solution for people who need a desk or meeting room. Computers and video conferencing equipment are available for hire.

Furniture includes typical office workstations in the work areas and meeting rooms and Philippe Starck-designed seating in the café. Every detail contributes to the impression of a functional and well-designed office. Even the infamous motorway services toilet has been upgraded with private wash facilities that would not be out of place in a quality hotel.

As a pioneer project, Workspace shows how motorway service stations can become destinations for work rather than just places to take a break within transport hubs. As a part of the nomadic work landscape, it provides alternative work environments for individuals or teams on the move, alongside the more obvious hotels that have been established at motorway junctions. Three such schemes have been built so far: at Heston, Reading and Leigh Delamere services in the UK. **location** UK **client** Granada Road Services **completed** 2000 **total floor space** 400 square metres (4,310 square feet)

1 Workspace reception
provides equipment
and office services
such as photocopying
and printing for
nomadic workers,
as well as support

2 View into Workspace
environment from
the main service
station concourse

3 A café-style area
called the Lounge
provides an informal
zone for work

4 Typical touchdown or
short-stay workstation
in the Hot Desk Zone,
where people pay a
fee to access the
space, technology
and facilities

Gallery-S
Mie, Japan
Hiroshi Kondo

228

IN A world of nomadic working, where ubiquitous computing means that anywhere you hang your hat can become your workstation, it is not surprising that architects and designers are exploring the idea of the dematerialized office. The final project in *21st Century Office* expresses just such an idea: Japanese designer Hiroshi Kondo plays with the theme of office as object that can be distilled into virtual nothingness – and then reconstructed to provide a physical environment.

The scheme is for a construction company, Sun refre, which wanted its new office in a typical Japanese residential suburb to draw attention to itself and entice creative clients to consider the company's services. Kondo's strategy was to design the space as a minimalist glass gallery suffused with light.

During the week, Gallery-S, as it is known, operates as an office, albeit a strictly paperless one. At weekends, the computers that make possible such a tidy and detritus-free workspace are removed to make room for an art gallery where the work of local residents is exhibited. The transparent surfaces of desks aid this remarkable transformation as the office literally disappears.

But just in case you might be led to believe that Gallery-S is an entirely futuristic project, Hiroshi Kondo also injects a sense of Japanese tradition into the Sun refre office with the use of *shoji*, simple sliding doors with rice-paper panels, to partition off smaller rooms within the space.

This is a timely reminder that Japanese designers have explored ideas of immateriality, lightness and transparency for centuries – and that the opportunities of the new digital age represent simply a new chapter in a long story.

location Mie, Japan **client** Sun refre **completed** 2000 **total floor space** 88 square metres (950 square feet)

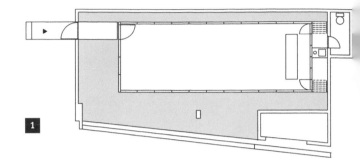

1

1 Floor plan

2 The Sun refre office
   is presented as a
   mysterious glass,
   light-filled box

3 Interior view shows
   transparent desks
   that become gallery
   plinths at weekends

FOLLOWING PAGES
4, 5
   The dematerializing
   office is a fitting
   symbol for a work-
   anywhere culture
   in which physical
   boundaries become
   increasingly
   meaningless

2

5

nomadic: Gallery-S

ALLSTEEL HEADQUARTERS
Muscatine, Iowa
architect Gensler **project team** Collin Burry (San Francisco, designer/interiors), Dian Duvall (San Francisco, design director/graphics), Lamar Johnson (Chicago, principal-in-charge), Bridget Mahoney-Farmer (New York, designer), Beth Novitsky (New York), Mark Shinn (Chicago), Stephen Katz (Chicago, job captain), Sophie Custer (Chicago, manager), Nao Etsuki (San Francisco), Janice Natchek (San Francisco, designer/ graphics), Masateru Yoshida (San Francisco), Elizabeth Uhlig (Chicago) **client** Allsteel Inc. **general contractor** Knutsen **furniture systems** Allsteel **terrace lighting** JS Nolan + Associates **mechanical engineer** KJWW

ANOTHER.COM
London, UK
architects Nowicka Stern **project team** Oded Stern-Meiraz, Marta Nowicka **client** another.com **project managers** European and Pacific **contractor** Mountbatten Contracts **turf specialists** Stafford and Sons **stools** Niva Contracts **task chair** Tsunami **filing cabinets/pedestals** Robert Webster **lighting** GFC Lighting

BEACON COMMUNICATIONS OFFICE
Meguro, Tokyo
concept design and project development Klein Dytham Architecture **project team** Astrid Klein, Mark Dytham, Shimpei Tokitsu, Tuko Iwamatsu, Hiroto Kubo **project collaborator** The Design Studio (project development and management) **project team** Stuart Kay, Shoji Koshimizu, Hiroshi Nagakura **client** Beacon Communications **consultation** DG Jones **project team** John Critchley, Toshikazu Yamamoto **main contractor** Takashimaya Space Creates

BLOOMBERG
London, UK
architecture and design Powell-Tuck Associates **client** Bloomberg LP **project coordinator** Ashford Property Services **mechanical and engineering consultants** The Engineering Practice **structural engineers** Whitby Bird & Partners Ltd **lighting design** DPA Lighting Consultants **communications consultant** Focus-3

building manager GVA Grimley **fire consultant** Jeremy Gardner Associates **audiovisual consultant** Mark Johnson Consultants **acoustics consultant** Sandy Brown Associates **furniture supply** SCP Contracts Ltd, Dovetail Contract Furniture **art consultants** Scarlet Projects **construction managers** Ibex Interiors Ltd **aquatic design** Aquatic Design Centre Ltd **architect (base build)** Foster & Partners

CELLULAR OPERATIONS HEADQUARTERS
Swindon, UK
architect Richard Hywel Evans Architecture and Design Ltd **project team** Richard Hywel Evans, Pietro Granaiola, Simon Leslie, Hayley Wade, Ric Voss **project management and quantity surveyor** E.C. Harris **structural engineer** Buro Happold **services engineer** Curona Design **main contractor** Tilbury Douglas **mechanical and electrical engineer** PBS **glass façade** Pilkington, Baco **daylight insulation** Oklux **blinds** Jet Blades Engineering **fit-out contractor** Cheshire Contracts **reception desk** ISM Design with Vale Cottage Motors **concrete stair** Patterns & Moulds **metalwork stair** Mitchell Gate **cladding** Euro Clad **lighting** Zumtobel **landscape** Elcotts **signage** Pierce Signs **revolving door** Boon Edam **sliding glass entry** Roll Trac **security** Nova Security **chilled beams** SAS **loose furniture** Connections Interiors Ltd **ironmongery** Allgoods

CLAYDON HEELEY JONES MASON ADVERTISING AGENCY
London, UK
architect Ushida Findlay **client** Claydon Heeley **main contractor** Interior plc (special works department) **service engineer** Fulcrum Consulting **quantity surveyor** Mike Porter Associates **acoustical consultant** Fulcrum Consulting **audiovisual consultant** Wave Ltd

CONCRETE MEDIA
New York, New York, USA
architect Specht Harpman **project team** Scott Specht, Louise Harpman (project designers), Rosemary Smith (project

manager) **client** Concrete Incorporated **consultant** Lilker Associates (MEP) **contractor** Manhattan Business Interiors **custom steel entrances and doors** Bliss Nor-Am **custom interior steel glazing, special hardware and surface** Millennium Steel **fibreglass partitions** Seal Fibreglass **wood cabinetry** NJS **cork wallcovering** Wicander **plastic laminate** Formica **raised access floor** Tri-State **hardware** Schlage, Stanley, Norton, Maglock

AV62 ARQUITECTOS OFFICE
Barcelona, Spain
architect AV62 Arquitectos SL **project team** Antonio Foraster, Victoria Garriga **client** AV62 Arquitectos SL **main contractor** Diss & Com SL **graphic design** PFP Disseny Gràfic **structural architects** Eskubi-Turró Arquitectes SL

DUFFY DESIGN
New York, New York, USA
architect MAP (Mahar Adjimi Partners) **client** Duffy Design **engineer** Goldman Copeland **lighting** Consultant Goldstick Lighting Design **furniture project management** Ferguson Cox Associates **general contractor** Lewis & Kennedy

DVD INNOVATION CENTRE NEW MEDIA AG
Dortmund, Germany
architect Planungsgruppe Drahtler GmbH **project team** Ulrich Drahtler, Britta Lehnhoff, Björn Nolte, Thorsten Schlockermann **client** Hildegard Lüke – Werner Wirsing-Lüke **main contractor** Freundlieb Bauunternehmung GmbH & Co **surveyor** Detlef Grave **collaborator** 3dpixel company gmbh; real ©ity virtual reality **garden and landscape architect** Paul Flender **house technology** Ingenieurgesellschaft Drücke

DZ BANK BUILDING
Berlin, Germany
architect Gehry Partners LLP **project team** Frank O. Gehry (design principal), Randy Jefferson (project principal), Craig Webb (project designer), Marc Salette, Tensho Takemori (project architects), Laurence Tighe, Eva Sobesky,

233

George Metzger, Jim Dayton, John Goldsmith, Jorg Ruegemer, Scott Uriu (projects members), Jeff Guga, Michael Jobes, Kirk Blaschke, Nida Chesonis, Tom Cody, Leigh Jerrard, Tadao Shimizu (model builders), Rick Smith, Bruce Shepard (computer modelling) **executive architect** Planungs AG – Neufert Mittmann Graf **project team** Michael Heggemann (project manager), Achim Hauser, Johannes Wilberz, Masoud Afchar **client** DG Immobilien Management GmbH, Hines Grundstucksentwicklung GmbH **structural engineers** Ingenieur Büro Müller Marl GmbH; Schlaich Bergermann und Partner **mechanical/electrical engineer** Brandi Ingenieure GmbH **façade consultant** Planungsbüro Für Ingenieurleistungen **lighting consultant** A.G. Licht **elevator consultant** Jappsen & Stanigier Berlin GmbH **acoustics** Audio Consulting Munich **audiovisual consultant** R.R. Ingenieurbüro Für Gebaudetechnik **kitchen consultant** Ingenieurbüro Schaller **fire safety consultant** Technische Prüfgesellschaft Lehmann **Italian limestone** Laboratorio Morseletto **skylight and atrium glazing** Josef Gartner and Co. **metal windows and entrances** Aepli **wood windows** Schindler **lighting** Erco, Zumtobel

EGG CALL CENTRE
Derby, UK
architects, interior designers, furniture consultants DEGW **client** Prudential Banking plc **project manager, quantity surveyor, construction manager, planning supervisor** Bucknall Austin **mechanical and electrical engineering consultants** ES Consulting **structural engineering consultant** John Nolan Associates **security consultant** B Prepared **acoustics consultant** University of Southampton **catering consultant** CDG

EXPOSURE PR (THIRD FLOOR)
London, UK
first phase: interior design Creneau International **project team** Will Erens, Fleur Paterson (concept design and customizing team), James Cameron, Gerry McDonnell (project management) **client** Exposure **main contractor** Classic Interiors Contractors Ltd **electrical contractor** Modern Electrical Contractors Ltd **heating and air handling** CCN Ltd **second phase: interior design/project management/quantity surveyor/main contractor/lighting consultant** Paul Daly

Design Services **project team** Luis Nheu, Paddy Austin (senior designers), Philip Dunford, Ambia Salam (designers), Phil Cheng (junior) **client** Exposure PR **graffiti** Ben Eine **photography** Carol Fulton

FOOTE, CONE & BELDING
Irvine, California, USA
architect/lighting design Clive Wilkinson Architects (CWA) **project team** Clive Wilkinson, Ian Macduff, Alexis Rappaport, Steve Lesko (project architect), Jonathan Chang, Anne Christensen, Christine Girone, Richard Hammond, James Kelly, Vance Ruppert, Ho-Yu Fong, Walter Mussachi, Bob Hsin, Catherine Garrison **client** Foote, Cone & Belding **client representative** Connie Kozlowski **project manager** Professional Real Estate Services (PRES) **structural engineer** KPFF Consulting Engineers **mechanical engineer** Tsuchiyama & Kaino **electrical engineer** OMB Electrical Engineers Inc. **landscape architect** Burton & Company **general contractor** Haskell Constructors Ltd **workstations** Sitag/D-Tank **custom rubber flooring** Johnsonite **custom dyed carpet** Design Weave **general millwork** Daystar **CWA custom millwork** J.T.I. **entrance lobby chairs** Herman Miller/'Chadwick' **custom 'sheep' couches** Orange/CWA **custom 'peanut' tables** Inside/CWA **clubhouse chairs** Aldo Ciabatti/'Ronde' **clubhouse tables** Knoll/'Propeller' **boardroom surfboard installation** DLC Surfboards **boardroom custom fibreglass table and audiovisual unit** DLC Surfboards/CWA **boardroom chairs** Vitra/'Meda' **conference room table** J.T.I. Millwork/CWA **conference room chairs** Knoll/ 'Sapper Executive' **Ping & Pong whiteboard-finished audiovisual units and conference table** J.T.I. Millwork; CMF Sheet Metal/CWA **custom coloured glass guardrail** Ocean Glass; Colour Pro **tent fabrication** J. Miller Canvas Inc. **ten chairs** Kartell/Philippe Starck 'Dr No'

FRITZSCH & MACKAT
Berlin, Germany
architect Mateja Mikulandra Mackat, Dipl.Ing. Architekten **client** Fritzsch & Mackat Advertising Agency **structural engineer** Ingenieurbüro Märschenz **acoustics** Consultant Michael Groß, Dipl.Ing **energy engineer** B & S Baupartner GmbH **electrical engineer** Klung & Partner GmbH **building site manager** Jörg Grünert, Dipl.Ing Architekt

FUKSAS (OFFICE OF MASSIMILANO FUKSAS)
Rome, Italy
architect Fuksas Associati **laminated steel furnishings** Fuksas Associati/Saporiti Italia **table and chairs** Massimilano and Doriana Fuksas

GALLERY-S
Mie, Japan
designer Hiroshi Kondo **client** Sun refre **consultants** Hiroshi Kondo **suppliers** Fujisato Kentikukoubou

GRANADA WORKSPACE
UK
architect BDG McColl **client** Granada Motorway Services **main contractor** Railstone Design **quantity surveyor** KMB **furniture** Hostess; Bene Office Furniture **lighting** Marlin **carpets** Milliken **partitions** Optima Partitioning Systems **ceramics** Floor Gres Ceramiche; Focus

HAPPY OFFICES (formerly Happy Forsman & Bodenfors AB)
Gothenburg, Sweden
architects White Arkitekter **project team** Per Bornstein, Mattias Lind (architects), Mathias Nilsson, Lars Zackrisson (engineers) **client/project manager** Krister Landberg Projektbyrå AB **project manager/real estate owner** Bygg Göta **contractor** Byggmästarna KB **ventilation** Velco AB **plumbing** Haga El & Rör AB **electricity** Gustafssons Elinstallationer AB **structure** BKN Konsult **painting** Winquist Måleri AB **textile carpets** Kasthall **rubber floor** Mondo **lighting** Fixtures Zero (work light), Europaljus/Sumtobel (spotlights), Abeta Belysning/ERCO (wallwashers), Flos (pendant lights) **fittings** Boxbeslag/FSB (door handles), Dorma (furniture) **furniture** Cappellini (upholstered chairs), Paustian (sofas), Bröderna Persson Specialsnickeri (custom-made furniture) **kitchen/bathroom appliances** Miele, Siemens, Hansgrohe (taps) **laminates** Abt Laminate **ceramic tiles** Marazzi **solid surfaces** Corian **ceramic mosaic** Villeroy & Boch

IBM E-BUSINESS INNOVATION CENTER
Santa Monica, California, USA
architect HOK (Hellmuth, Obata + Kassabaum Inc.) **project team** Susan Grossinger (principal-in-charge), Brett Schwery, CID (project manager), Barbara

Ostroff (senior project designer), Louis Bretana (job captain), Steven Drucker (design principal), Dorota Urbans (designer) **client** IBM **main contractor** The Beck Group **mechanical engineer** The Sullivan Partnership **electrical engineer** V&M Engineering **audiovisual consultant** Advanced Media Design **lighting consultant** Patrick B. Quigley Associates **metallic ceiling baffles and acoustical wood panels** Decoustics **ceiling systems** USG **wood flooring** Permagrain **vinyl flooring** Lonseal **lighting** Leucos **acrylic panels** Light Blocks **shag area carpets** Decorative Carpets **patterned carpets** Bentley Carpets **casegoods furniture** Fantoni **accent seating** Knoll Studio **currents systems furniture** Knoll

INSTITUTE OF DIRECTORS' HEADQUARTERS London, UK
design hemingwaydesign **project team** Gerardine Hemingway (project manager), Wayne Hemingway **client** Institute of Directors **main contractor** P.D. Everett Building; BGH Joinery **furniture** CA1 (A Frame Range), Moroso (Steel Range – Atrivm), Montis (Viaduct), Hitch Mylius (sofas) **upholstery** Daily News Range – NoNo **carpets** Milliken – Go Modular designed by hemingwaydesign **mural** Robin Whitmore **other art pieces** Gerardine Hemingway **washbasins** Durat **lighting** Gusto (stairwell), sputnik (reception) **taps** Vola

INTERNET HOME
Milan, Italy
concept design The Studio & Partners **project team** Torsten Fritze, Luca Azzoni **collaborator** Progetto CMR **client** Cisco Systems **participating companies** Ariston Digital Wrap, BTicino, Cisco Systems, Luceplan, Molteni, Unifor, Dada **furnishings** Dada (kitchen), Duravit (ceramics), Estel (office), Friz Hansen (seating), Hoesch (bathtub), HP (pc), Luceplan (lighting), Molteni & Co. (furniture), MEC (pc), Seleco (colour TV), Stone Italiana (flooring), Unifor (doors)

ISSEY MIYAKE INC. HEADQUARTERS
Tomigaya shibuya-ku, Tokyo, Japan
architect Kajima Design **client** Itochu Corporation **contractor** Kajima Corporation **interior and furniture design** Christian Biecher; H.A. Deux.

MCKINSEY & COMPANY HEADQUARTERS
Amsterdam, The Netherlands
office concept Veldhoen + Company **interior architect** Bruls en Co **client** McKinsey & Company **project manangement** PKB Bouwadviseurs **interior contractor** Soons Interieurbouw b.v. **technical installation advisor** Huisman en van Muijen **e-installations** Imtech Projects **installation contractor** Stork Installatietechniek b.v.; Imtech Projects **security installation contractor** Nedap Secure b.v. **acoustics advisor** Adviesbureau Peutz & Associés b.v. **lighting consultant** Adviesbureau Peutz & Associé b.v.

MEDIA PLAZA
Utrecht, The Netherlands
architect Sander Architekten **project team** Ellen Sander, Baukje van der Steeg, Jay McGill **client organization** Media Plaza **main contractor** HBG **artist team** Wilma Kuil, Eric Staller **special furniture** Bosman Interieurbouw (Interior builder), Karma Design **furniture** SV Interieur, CAR Furniture, Wonen 2000 **light** Bossinade Lightworks, Modular Lighting Instruments **walls/ceiling/auditorium/sound control** Coverall **mechanical and electrical contractor** Kropman

MERCADERS BUILDING
Barcelona, Spain
architect and interior designers Enric Miralles and Benedetta Tagliabue **client** Enric Miralles and Benedetta Tagliabue **main contractor** Tierra y Mar SA **general contractor** Interabarca **structural system/metal** Esteve Miret, Estmart **landscape architects** Jardineria Moix, Enric Miralles, Benedetta Tagliabue **quantity surveyor** Jordi Altes **structure** R. Brufau **wood carpenter** J. Figueras

MUZAK CORPORATE HEADQUARTERS
Fort Mill, South Carolina, USA
architects Pentagram **project team** James Biber (partner/architect), Michael Zweck-Bronner (associate/architect), Kit Hinrichs (partner/graphics), Brian Jacobs (associate/graphics) **collaborators** Little & Associates, Architects **project team** Ruth Cline, Michael Coates **client** Muzak **structural engineer** David Walker Engineering **mechanical and electrical**

engineer Little & Associates Architects **general contractor and construction management** Bovis Lend Lease **acoustics** Grover Meetze, Jr. **furniture dealer** Vitra **signage** Pentagram **flooring** Rigidized Metal Corp **carpet** Lees **ceiling** Tectum **lighting** Lithonia and General Electric **window frames/wall systems** Acoustical **workstations** Vitra; Haworth **workstation seating** Herman Miller **cafeteria/dining/auditorium seatlng** Gordon International **upholstery** DesignTex **tables** Vitra; Haworth **files** Office Speciality **elevators** Thyssen Dover Elevators **HVAC** United Mechanical **access flooring** Tate Access Floors

OCUBIS SERVICED OFFICES
London, UK
architect Magyar Marsoni Architects **project team** David Magyar, Alvise Marsoni, Zoltan Szotyori, Xaver Moll, Salwa Heath **client** Ocubis Serviced Offices **structural engineer and planning supervisor** Fidler Associates **main contractor** Ocubis **subcontractors** Pollards Fyrespan (glass and steel stair and 'box') **suppliers** Kirkstone Quarries (slate)

OGILVY & MATHER HEADQUARTERS
Culver City, California, USA
architect Shubin + Donaldson Architects **project team** Russell Shubin, Robin Donaldson (partners), Sean Hagan, (project architect/manager), Josh Blumer (project architect), Fred Besancon, Mark Gee, Mina Javid, Rob Sutman, Mahyar Abousaeedi, Mark Hershman, Brennan Linder **meeting/gathering space in collaboration with** Eric Owen Moss **shell and core architect** Eric Owen Moss **client** Ogilvy & Mather **general contractor** Sierra Pacific Constructors, Inc. **lighting consultant** Lighting Design Alliance **mechanical engineer** Fruchtman & Associates Inc. **electrical engineer** Paul Immerman PE **perforated metal tube material** Custom Fabrication by Weiss Sheet Metal Company **carpeting** Masland Contract **paintwork** Sinclair Paints **supergraphics** Imagic **metal sliding doors** dTank-manufactured by Sitag **laminate** Formica **lighting suppliers** Canlet, Stonco, Prudential, Prescolite, Gotham, Bruck, Lithonia, Alkco Desk Chairs Herman Miller **kitchen stool** Sitag **all other furniture** Custom by Shubin + Donaldson, manufactured by Sitag

OLIVA-REMOLÀ ARCHITECT STUDIO,
Barcelona, Spain
architects Amadeu Oliva i Uriel **project team** Maria Rosa Remolà i Ferrer (master builder) **client** Amadeu Oliva i Uriel and Maria Rosa Remolà i Ferrer **concrete structure** Ferrallados Asis **bricklaying** Novapolis SL **plumbing** Fontaneria Terrassa SL **electricity** Armengol Serveis Electrics SL **refrigeration** Reinfred SL **elevator** EBYP SA **carpenter** Anco **concrete pavement** Lotum Regeneracion Industrial **wool work** Cobra Instalaciones y Servicios **iron** Cerrajeria Natalio SL **painter** Serena **wood furniture** Amadeu Oliva i Uriel (design), Vicmor, SCP (manufacturer) **chairs** Oscar Tusquets (design), Casas (manufacturer)

OLIVER, WYMAN & COMPANY
New York, New York, USA
architect Resolution 4 Architecture **project team** Joseph Tanney, Robert Luntz (company directors), Catarina Ferreira (project architect), Tetsuya Yamazaki, Steven Chua, Michael Sweebe, Eric Fauerbach, David Freeland, Melanie Smith, Dan Piselli **contractor** CP Construction

PHILIPP AND KEUNTJE ADVERTISING AGENCY
Hamburg, Germany
architect feldmann + schultchen design **project team** André Feldmann, Arne Jacob Schultchen (principals-in-charge), Stephan Kremerskothen (project director) **client** Philipp und Keuntje Werbeagentur GmbH, Hamburg **main contractor** Marschner & Krogmann (woodworks) **furniture** feldmann + scultchen (design), Marschner & Krogmann (fabrication) **lighting** feldman + schultchen (design), Keppler & Schulz (fabrication) **electrical** wyso GmbH **walls** Ropa Generalbau GmbH **flooring** Gätje Natursteinwerk GmbH & Co (terrazzo), Cengiz (carpet) **heating** Maue & Becker GmbH
air conditioning Kälte Bast GmbH **statics** Ingenieurbüro Sander

QUIKSILVER CORPORATE HEADQUARTERS
Newport Beach, California, USA
architect Bauer and Wiley Architects **project team** Jay S. Bauer, Annette Wiley **client** Quiksilver Inc. **main contractor** Inner Space Constructors **structural engineer** Johnson & Neilsen Associates MEP Engineer P2S Engineering **lighting** Francis

Krahe & Associates **acoustics and audiovisual consultants** Marshall Long Acoustics **costings** Cumming LLC **millwork** Artcrafters **workstations** Herman Miller **laminate** Nevamar **linoleum flooring** Forbo **bamboo flooring** Plyboo **lumasite** American Acrylic Corporation **carpet** Interface **Starck chairs** Driade

REALNAMES CORPORATION OFFICES
San Carlos, California, USA
architect Blauel Architects **project team** Andy Nettleton (project architect), Peter Jurschitzka, Robert Zeller, Bernhard Blauel **collaborator** Cindy Davis (Devcon) **client** RealNames Corporation, San Carlos, CA **contractor** Devcon Construction Inc. **flooring** Tufflex **workstations** Teknicon **electrics and lighting** Frank Electric **lights** Zumtobel

REALNAMES CORPORATION OFFICES 2
Red Wood Shores, California, USA
architect Blauel Architects **project team** Peter Jurschitzka, Angelika Zwingel, Robert Zeller, Bernhard Blauel **collaborators** Davis Larsen, Dimple Mittal, Robert Hayes of Bottom Duvivier Design and Architecture **client** RealNames Corporation, San Carlos CA **general contractor** DPR Construction Inc. **design/build mechanical** Air Sheet Metal Inc. **design/build electrical** Palmer Electric

REEBOK HEADQUARTERS
Canton, Massachusetts, USA
architect NBBJ **project team** Scott Wyatt (partner-in-charge), Steve McConnell (design principal-in-chief), K. Robert Swartz (principal-in-charge), Jonathan Ward (senior project designer), Nick Charles (senior technical architect), Jin Ah Park (project designer), Ruben Gonzalez (construction administration lead), Chris Larson (senior project designer – interiors), Alan Young (senior project designer – interiors), Dave Burger (senior technical architect – interiors) **client** Reebok International Ltd **structural engineer** McNamara Salvia **mechanical/electrical engineer** Cosentini Associates **general contractor/ construction manager** Turner/O'Connor Joint Venture **curtain wall** Advanced Structures Inc. (designer); Karas & Karas Glass Co. (manufacturer) **exterior metal panels** Alusuisse Composites **architectural precast panels** Bretons Prefabriques DuLac **exterior glazing** Viracon **wall**

insulation Roxul **roof system** Firestone **elevators** Otis Elevator Co. **energy management controls** Siemenes **plumbing fixtures** American Standard **wood doors** Eggers Industries **door hardware** Hagar, Yale, Norton **ceilings** Hunter Douglas **flooring** Mondo **office furniture** Steelcase.

SONY HEADQUARTERS
London, UK
architect Fletcher Priest Architects **project team** Antonia Infanger, Ruth Londsdale, Allan Poulter, Keith Priest, Gerry Whale **client** Sony Computer Entertainment Europe **project manager** APS Project Management **consulting engineer** Dewhurst MacFarlane **services engineer** Ernest Griffiths & Sons **cost consultants** APS Project Management; Stephens & Co **contractor** Dean + Bowes **IT consultant** Secom **shell architect** Tate & Hindle Design **carpet** Interface **timber access** Floor Hewetson **lighting** Erco (lower ground floor); Modular Lighting (reception and boardroom); Ross Lovegrove (interview room); Sill (floor uplighter); LucePlan (sixth floor meeting room); Fletcher Priest/Light Zone (lighting of reception wall and desk) **lower ground floor movable walls** Hüppe **workstations** Vitra **partitions** Optima **furniture** Bramwell (cabinets); Ron Arad (reception chairs); Ron Arad/Kartell (plastic elastic chairs); Nigel Coates/Hitch Mylius (Oxo chairs); Wilkahn (folding meeting table); Vitra (meeting room chairs); Fletcher Priest custom made (all other furniture).

TBWA\CHIAT\DAY
Los Angeles, USA
architect Clive Wilkinson Architects (CWA) **project team** Clive Wilkinson (design director), John Berry, Robert Kerr (project architects), Jane Wuu, Christian Nandi, Tom Nohr, Mark Hudson, Andrea Keller, Marni Nelco, Ho-Yu Fong **client** TBWA\Chiat\Day **general contractor** Matt Construction **project manager** Stegeman & Kastner **structural engineer** John A Martin & Associates **MEP engineers** Syska & Hennessy **lighting design** Joe Kaplan **tent fabrication** J. Miller Canvas **rubber flooring** Burke Roleau **custom dyed carpet** Shaw Industries **park furniture** Smith & Hawkin **millwork** Daystar, Pat Abarta **workstations** Steelcase/Turnstone (designed by Clive Wilkinson) **lighting/Oz conference room** Fuscia (designed by A. Castiglioni and

manufactured by Flos) **boardroom chairs** Onda (manufactured by Vitra) **surfboard bar** Spyder Boards **gatehouse chairs** Bibendum (designed by Eileen Gray and manufactured by Palazzetti)

TELEWORKING VILLAGE
Colletta di Castelbianco, Liguria, Italy
architect Giancarlo De Carlo **project manager** Realinvest International Real Estate (other credits not available at time of going to print)

TOYOTA OFFICES
Epsom Downs, Surrey, UK
architecture, interior design and planning Sheppard Robson **project team** Tim Evans (partner), Philip Doyle (project architect), Rodi MacArthur, Ed Jackson, Rupert Evers, Michael Chadwick, Frank Peacock, Fred Renton, Tom Alexander, Barry Kendell. Interiors Glenn Vaus, Mark Thompson, Lara Ford, Hannah Fodden **client** Toyota **property consultant** Insignia Richard Ellis **consulting engineers** Ove Arup & Partners **engineers** Whitby Bird & Partners **chartered quantity surveyors** David Langdon & Everest **masterplanning, landscape architecture, planning** Derek Lovejoy Partnership **fire engineering** Jeremy Gardiner Associates **furniture** Mott Associates **contractor** Takenaka **selected sub-contractors and suppliers: concrete structure** Duffy Construction **structural steel** Archbell Greenwood Structures; DGT Fabrications **bolted glass wall and glazed roof** Space Decks **curtain walling** Structal **brise soleil** Taurus Littrow **carpet and vinyl** Prospect & Peachgate **ceramic tiles** Harper & Edwards

VALTECH
London, UK
architect Harper Mackay **director-in-charge** Stephen Archer **client** Valtech **main contractor** Ibex Interiors **quantity surveyor** Jackson Coles **structural engineers** Price & Myers **freeholder** Bee Bee Developments **mechanical contractor** Mala **mechanical consultant** John Brady

Associates **approved inspector** JHA Ltd **sub-contractors** Lensvelt (furniture); Clear Direction (signage); Swan Graphics (image walls).

VIRGIN LOUNGE, JFK
New York, New York, USA
lead design consultant Patrick Hegarty, W1 Studio **Virgin Atlantic design manager** Dee Cooper **architect** TsAO and Mckown **client** Virgin Atlantic **contractor** VRH Construction Corp. **code consultant** STDI Consulting Group Inc. **cost estimator** Cost Concepts, Inc. **lighting consultant** Design One Corporation **structural consultant** Severud Associates **MEP consultant** John J. Guth PE **kitchen consultant** American Kitchen Associates Inc. **audiovisual/acoustics consultant** Shen Milsom & Wilke, Inc. **furniture agent** Invoke Ltd FF&E Manufacturer Benchmark **art consultant** Carey Ellis Company

VITRA OFFICES
Weil am Rhein, Germany
architect, interior design and lighting design SPGA (Sevil Peach Gence Associates) **project team** Ken Allison, Sebastian Avendano, Peter Crompton, Sevil Peach, Gary Turnbill, Craig Welch **client** Vitra **building contractor** Mönch Wilhelm Bauunternehmung GmbH & Co KG **mechanical engineer** Bühler **acoustics engineer** Genest & Partner **acoustic panels** Sto AG, Ecophon, Wolfgang Steinecke **timber and metal floor/umbrella hangers with air conditioning** Instech Installationstechnik **joinery contractor** Baumgartner GmbH Einrichtungen patio contractor Haring Fenster & Fassaden AG **lighting consultant and supplier** Ansorg GmbH **soft lighting** Suppliers Flos, Luceplan, Artemide **curtain fabric** Création Baumann GmbH **rugs** Ruckstuhl AG Teppichfabrick **painting and concrete floor** Stern and Richwalski **rooflights** Aluform Alucobondverarbeitungs GmbH **roofwork** Jauslin GmbH **electrical installation** Bieg

Hermann & Sohn Elektrotechnisches Unternehmen GmbH **statics engineer** Müller und Klein **sun blinds** Eckert Sonenschutzsysteme **landscape** Schmitt Gärtnerei **hanging canvas panels production and installation** Hügle GmbH Bau- u. Möbelschreinerei **glass for office doors** Pilkington Flachglasag

WESTFERRY ROAD LIVE/WORK STUDIOS
London, UK
architect CZWG Architects **project designer** J. Corcoram **client** Peabody Trust **contractor** Gleesons Design & Build **quantity surveyor** Davies Langdon & Everest **structural and mechanical engineers** Whitby Bird

WINSTAR E.CENTER
New York, New York, USA
principal architect Graham Hanson Design (formerly Hanson Carlson) **project team** Graham Hanson (principal), Yuji Yamakazi, Chris Dimaggio **architect of record** Mancini-Duffy **client** Winstar Communications Inc. **project management** Kendra Carlson **lighting designer** Syska & Hennessy Lighting Design Group **fabrication and audiovisual integration** Rathe Productions **MEP engineer** Edwards & Zuck **lighting consultant** Syska & Hennessey **construction management** Plaza Construction Corporation **technology systems consultant** ViaGate Technologies

THE ZONE@ PRICEWATERHOUSECOOPERS
Philadelphia, USA
architect Gensler **project team** Diane Hoskins, Janet Pogue, Chris Banks, Marc Parsons, Ehren Gaag, Anne Runow, Patrick Brady, John Lowe, Pam Holland-Hynes **client** PricewaterhouseCoopers **MEP engineer** HF Lenz **lighting** Johnson-Schwinghammer **audiovisual** Vistacom **contractor** Clemens Construction **speciality glass** Wallach Glass Studio **furniture** Beaux Art Group (Knoll); Office Pavilion (Herman Miller)

index

Index of architects, designers,projects and places

The publisher would like to thank the following sources for permission to use their images.

Ramus Amruth (34–39); Christopher Barrett/Hedrich Blessing (74–77); Felix Borkenau/artur (84, 126–129); Tom Bonner (16, 28–33); Richard Bryant/ARCAID (198, 214–217); Benny Chan/Fotoworks (132–137, 192–197); David Churchill (184–187); Peter Cook/VIEW (219–220); Guy Drayton (149, 152 top left and bottom); Chris Gascoigne/VIEW (24–27, 96–99, 174–179); Dennis Gilbert/VIEW (120–125, 224–225); Karin Heßmann/artur (188–191); Chris Hollick (56–61); Werner Huthmacher/artur (154–157); Timothy Hursley (66–71); Nick Ivins (138–141); Takao Kato (228–231); Katsuhisa Kida (45–47 bottom); Ola Kjelbye (142–147); Kenji Kobayashi (44); Waltraud Krase (48 top); John Edward Linden/ARCAID (18–23); Scott MacDonald/Hedrich Blessing (90–95, 116–119); Ray Main (200–205); Duccio Malagamba (62–65, 207); Peter Mauss/ESTO (40–43); John Ian McLean (162–167); Michal Moran (158–161); John O'Brian (226–227); Giovanna Piemonti (72–73); Eugeni Pons (180–183, 209); Andrew Putler (210–213); Courtesy Realinvest (222); Christian Richters (48, 49–53); Kozo Takayama (130, 168–173); Alexander van Berge (110–115); Morley von Sternberg (78–83); Paul Warchol (54–55, 100–109); James Winspear (150–151, 152 top right); Yasuaki Yoshinaga (47 top); Kim Zwarts (86–89)

Authors' acknowledgements

Jeremy Myerson gives special thanks to Matthew and Nathan Myerson for their support.

Philip Ross would like to acknowledge the assistance and support of everyone who has helped him formulate ideas for the future and the workplace; Michelle van Vuuren at UNWIRED; and particularly Katy Manuel for all her help and support, and Oliver Ross for his inspiration.

240